Mary tells of her strug_____ that was spiraling her towa_____ despair and hopelessness as _____ ᵤᵤough the medical community and her own efforts. She struggled just to survive, like the shrub planted in the desert (Jeremiah 17:6). It was not until she discovered Jesus the Healer that hope and renewal came forth. Once she turned herself over to Him, the Lord led her every step of the way to complete restoration. Then she began to thrive and bear fruit, like the tree planted by the waters (Jeremiah 17:8). Scriptural principles that are necessary for anyone seeking their own healing come alive as they are interwoven within the story and their effects are made evident. She shows that when we depend on our own devices and the works of man, our lives are fruitless, but when we turn to God and place our dependence on Him the impossible suddenly becomes possible. Mary includes many keys to receiving healing that the Holy Spirit taught her on her journey of discovering that Jesus heals today. She gives God all the glory as the story of how the Lord pursued and rescued her unfolds.

Mary also has the distinction of being related to President Harry S. Truman. She speaks of her great-uncle as a Christian man of faith who believed in prayer and sought the leading of God in his life. She tells how Harry Truman understood some of the Old Testament prophecies about the regathering of Israel in the End Times when he recognized and supported Israel in 1948.

It is clear that it is Mary's desire to help others by sharing what she learned. Her story is inspiring and informative. It is my expectation that many will be healed from the information in this book.

—MIKE BICKLE, DIRECTOR
INTERNATIONAL HOUSE OF PRAYER
KANSAS CITY, MO

Mary Gracey is a woman of God. She loves prayer, she loves people, and she has an unusual amount of faith to believe God for His presence and His power to touch those with pain in their bodies and in their hearts. Her story will be a great encouragement to you.

—FLOYD McCLUNG
SENIOR PASTOR, METRO CHRISTIAN FELLOWSHIP
KANSAS CITY, MO
FORMER INTERNATIONAL DIRECTOR OF
YOUTH WITH A MISSION (YWAM)
PRESIDENT OF ALL NATIONS TRAINING CENTER (ANTC)

HE LIFTED ME UP

Mary Truman Gracey

CREATION
HOUSE PRESS
A STRANG COMPANY

HE LIFTED ME UP
by Mary Truman Gracey
Published by Creation House Press
A Strang Company
600 Rinehart Road
Lake Mary, Florida 32746
www.creationhouse.com

Unless otherwise identified, Scripture quotations are from the King James Version of the Bible.

Scripture quotations marked NKJV are from the New King James Version of the Bible. Copyright © 1979, 1980, 1982, 1992 by Thomas Nelson, Inc., publishers.

Scripture quotations marked NAB are from the New American Bible. Copyright © 1969, 1986, 1987, 1991 by Catholic Bible Press, a division of Thomas Nelson Publishers.

Scripture quotations marked NASB are from the New American Standard Bible, and those marked NIV are from the New International Version of the Bible. These quotations were taken from the Comparative Study Bible, Revised Edition. Copyright © 1999 by The Zondervan Corporation.

Cover design by Terry Clifton
Interior design by David Bilby

Library of Congress Control Number: 2004100334
International Standard Book Number: 1-59185-548-9

04   05   06   07   08 — 9 8 7 6 5 4 3 2 1
Printed in the United States of America

DEDICATION

I want to dedicate this book to my wonderful husband, Joe. I thank him for always being there for me. He went above and beyond what anyone would have expected. I used to tell my mother that I wanted to marry a man with faithfulness and integrity like my father. God granted me that desire of my heart. I am also thankful for all of his excellent work and suggestions regarding this book.

Humble yourself in the sight of the Lord, and He will lift you up.

—JAMES 4:10

ACKNOWLEDGMENTS

I thank my daughter, Terri, for her sacrifices, for being there when I needed her, and for doing all that she could.

I am forever grateful to my sister, Rita, who was and is faithful. She and her husband, Carl Moser, are people I can always depend on. I thank Carl who sacrificed his time and labor many times over many years.

I am also grateful for the family God blessed me with. When I was so ill, they stood by me, helped me whenever they could, and did what was asked of them.

A special thanks to friends Larry and Stacia Bolz from whom I have learned many important truths. I appreciate the time Larry spent reading my manuscript and giving helpful suggestions and also Stacia's encouragement and positive input.

CONTENTS

PART III: BIBLE PRINCIPLES AFFECTING HEALING

APPENDICES

FOREWORD

At Marah, God revealed Himself to Israel as Jehovah Rapha—the Lord the Healer. (See Exodus 15:26.) The revelation is a picture of the cross being cast into the midst of human existence, revealing God's provision of freedom from the misery of sickness and disease through the death of Christ. Promises throughout the Old Testament reinforce this revelation of the mercy and kindness of God.

In the fullness of time the Word of God clothed Himself with flesh and demonstrated this revealed characteristic of the divine nature by "healing all manner of disease and all manner of sickness among the people" (Matt. 4:23). His mercy and compassion towards those who were sick is revealed throughout the Gospels. On one occasion, a leper came and fell at His feet and said, "If thou wilt, thou canst make me clean" (Mark 1:40). Jesus' response was immediate. Moved with compassion over the man's condition, He declared, "I will, be thou clean" (Mark 1:41).

The Book of Hebrews declares that this Jesus is "the same, yesterday, today, and forever" (Heb. 13:8). Therefore we can have an expectation in our day that we will experience an abundance of healings and miracles as our healing God continues to do what He has always done.

This is a story of an ordinary person experiencing God's mercy and kindness. It is the story of a woman, who, like the woman with the issue of blood, would not be denied, but instead overcame significant difficulties to reach out and touch the hem of Jesus' garment and in so doing received healing. (See Matthew 9:20–22.) However, this is more than a story; it is an exciting testimony that will encourage many who find themselves in the grip of some sickness or disease.

At many points along the way, Mary could have surrendered her hope and joined the ranks of those who have failed to obtain the promises because of their lack of endurance. Her determination and trust in the promises of God caused her to inherit, through faith and patience, the reward she sought. Rarely, however, are these battles won alone. The resolute support of her husband, Joseph, and others in the body of Christ helped her through the dark valleys that threatened to overcome her faith. So should the church be—a community of faith and encouragement rather than one of doubt and unbelief. The lack of such support has robbed many of their promised inheritance.

Mary and Joseph Gracey are precious people who, having once experienced the mercy and kindness of the Lord, now give themselves weekly to ministering to the many sick and infirm who travel to the Healing Rooms at the International House of Prayer in Kansas City, Missouri. Their compassion for the sick, their ministry, and their encouragement to persevere are tools in the hand of the Savior, releasing blessings to many.

It is my joy to recommend this volume, knowing that Mary's story will inspire and encourage you. It is my prayer that through this testimony you might be encouraged to obtain your inheritance and encounter the Healer yourself.

—KEVIN J. MATTHEWS
DIRECTOR OF HEALING AND PROPHETIC MINISTRIES
INTERNATIONAL HOUSE OF PRAYER, KANSAS CITY

INTRODUCTION

A life of hopelessness and despair is what I had been living for years. Through the years I had numerous things happen to me including some very serious, "incurable" health problems. I had no idea that Jesus healed today or was even involved in our lives. I was so far from where I needed to be it is a miracle that I heard the truth that was finally spoken to me, or that I received it even in a small way. But God, in His great compassion, mercy, and love, lifted me out of all of it. He changed my life from one of hopelessness and despair to one of health and great blessings. As my story unfolded, I discovered not only how to appropriate God's healing power in my own life, but also many Scriptural principles that anyone who seeks healing can apply to themselves. These discoveries are interwoven throughout the pages of this book. If you have tried the man-made solutions without success, I suggest an alternative—turn your problem over to the Manufacturer.

I came from an exceptional family. I had a wonderful mother and father who loved all of their six children. We were rich in family love, loyalty, and security. My father and his whole family were Protestants. My mother was Catholic as was her entire side of the family for many generations. I was raised in the Catholic Church and went to Catholic schools, where I received a good education. Growing up, I was taught to keep God's commandments and to do what was right. I was taught that Jesus was our Lord and Savior, that He had died on the Cross for our sins, and that He rose from the dead and will come again to judge the living and the dead. I was taught forgiveness of sin and life everlasting. I was told that God loved us. The Mass on Sunday was reverent, with readings from the Scriptures, beautiful music, a sermon, and communion. I was happy with my religion and was not searching for anything else.

1

HE LIFTED ME UP

My people are destroyed for lack of knowledge.

—HOSEA 4:6

Because I had not read or studied the Scriptures, I had very little knowledge of how to live my life in victory. I did not know about all of God's promises.

- ✝ I did not know how to hear from God, and I did not know that anyone heard from God.

- ✝ I did not know I was supposed to "surrender" myself to His will and that my life was to be lived for Him.

- ✝ I did not know that when you surrendered, gave your life to Jesus, and accepted Him into your heart the Holy Spirit came into your life in a new and more powerful way.

- ✝ I did not know that God spoke to us today like He spoke to people in the Bible.

- ✝ I did not know about the leading of the Holy Spirit.

- ✝ I definitely did not know anything about prophecy or the other gifts of the Holy Spirit. (See 1 Corinthians 12:7.)

- ✝ I did not know that Jesus heals physical and emotional diseases today the same as He did two thousand years ago. "Jesus Christ the same yesterday, and today and forever" (Heb. 13:8).

Because I had not read or studied God's Word, I did not know how much I did not know.

I discovered that if we do not know the Word of God we do not know much. We are lacking many important truths. The Bible, God's Holy Word, provides the real answers, the real truth, and the blueprint for living our lives in love, victory, health, and happiness. The Word of God is alive and powerful. I have now seen the truth of the Word work in my life and in the lives of others. Blessings have come from it.

2

Introduction

A Special Family Privilege

My childhood was fairly normal. I grew up in Independence, Missouri, just east of Kansas City. I was surrounded by grandparents, aunts, uncles, cousins, and many friends. We had a very large, busy family. Our parents treated all of us in a special way. As a teacher once told my mother, "You treat all your children as if each one was an only child." I grew up with a father who loved me and set good examples with teachings on integrity, honesty, and keeping your word. If you promised it, you did it, no matter what the cost. He was quick with a compliment and letting me know how much he trusted me. Those attitudes made me want to never disappoint him or violate the trust he had in me.

Every Sunday after church, my parents, brothers, and sisters climbed into the car for the forty-minute drive to Grandview, Missouri, to visit my grandparents. They had a large working farm near what is now the Truman Corners Shopping Center on Blue Ridge Boulevard near US-71 Highway. My grandfather was John Vivian Truman, the brother of Harry S. Truman, who, when I was a young child, was President of the United States. Children in school would occasionally ask me how it felt to be related to a president. I said I did not know how it felt not to be.

Harry S. Truman and his brother, Vivian (Mary's grandfather), in a motorcade during the Truman presidency. The inscription, in her uncle Harry's handwriting, was written to Mary's parents, J. C. and Mary Truman, in 1964.

3

Staying in the White House

Coming from a famous family, we did have a few privileges. One of those was staying at the White House with my parents, brother, and two sisters for almost a week when I was in grade school. One summer my father, who at that time worked for the National Archives, was called to Washington to attend some working sessions. So Uncle Harry invited us to stay at the White House. In his letter to my father, Uncle Harry told him not to make any hotel reservations. He said he would be there by himself and had about forty extra rooms! He was happy to have the company as Aunt Bess was in Independence at the time. We were all very excited and knew it was a great privilege that most people did not have. During our visit, my parents stayed in the Lincoln bedroom while my sister, Rita, and I shared a room close by. When we returned from site-seeing everyday, our beds would be turned down, with a bowl of fresh fruit and a silver pitcher of cold water on the nightstand. We were impressed and felt very special.

We ate breakfast on the Truman balcony with Uncle Harry and were introduced to finger bowls for our use after eating. I remember wondering what that little bowl of water with a lemon floating in it was for. I waited and watched and then followed my Uncle's example.

He made sure we were comfortable and saw all the sites while we were there. I remember being chauffeured around to different places, including the Supreme Court. Uncle Harry had each one of us sit in the Chief Justice's chair. He said someday we would be able to tell our children we had done this. While my dad went to work each day my mother had her hands full with the four of us. Mother was also pregnant with her fifth. The car we rode in each day had electric windows and controls that we were not used to. There also was a glass partition that could be raised between the back seat and the driver for privacy. As we traveled down the Washington streets, we would be constantly pressing buttons sending windows up and down and the glass partition up and down between us and the driver. The driver never said a word over our activities, but Mother discouraged us from our newfound fun.

4

Introduction

On one very hot, sunny day our cousin, Margaret Truman, drove us around town in a beautiful convertible with the top down. I sat in the front seat between Margaret and my mother. This was a special day with Margaret driving us to Mount Vernon. These were wonderful privileges we were experiencing, and we were grateful. We were filled with excitement for each day's activities.

After lunch each day my mother liked for us to have some quiet time before we ventured out for more sightseeing. Rita and I were left to our imaginations on the upper floor of the White House near our bedroom. On one side of a large open area, there were elevated French doors with a few steps on each side leading up to the doors. A short walkway connected the two sets of stairs. We pretended that this area was a stage. We took turns performing for each other, singing and dancing our way up and down the steps and across the walkway in front of the doors. That entertained us for a while. Then we tried the doors, not really expecting to open them. We were surprised and excited as they swung open. We quickly stepped outside onto a narrow space where we could stand. We were surrounded by pillars, but could look out over the White House grounds. As I looked down, I noticed that we were very high, and I felt uneasy. It would have been possible for a careless child to fall from that area. It definitely was no place for children. We knew we should not have been out there, so we did not stay long, as we did not want to get caught and get into trouble. We slipped back inside and shut the doors.

The next afternoon we did our usual performing on our make-believe stage and when we tired of that we tried to open the French doors again. We were disappointed to find them locked. Even though no one had said a word to us, we felt someone, maybe the Secret Service, had seen us, and had quickly and quietly eliminated a dangerous situation. Later my Father said we were seen kneeling down and peering through the pillars around the lower part of the railing. It seems that one of the butlers had locked the French doors leading outside.

When I see pictures of the White House today, it amazes me to see that the pillars are so close to the roof and that we were at no small risk. I doubt that very many White House guests have been out there—but we were!

The family had lunch one afternoon on the presidential yacht, *Williamsberg*. I will never forget all the military lined up in their white uniforms, standing at attention, while Uncle Harry, with us following, boarded the yacht for an exceptional lunch.

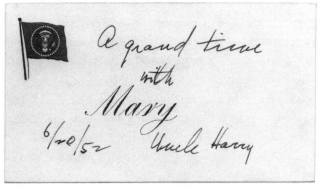

Mary's place card from lunch on the *Williamsberg*, autographed by Uncle Harry.

My parents knew Rose Conway, Uncle Harry's secretary, long before she went to Washington as his private secretary. During our stay at the White House, she came upstairs occasionally to see if we were being properly cared for.

Uncle Harry invited us to watch a movie (a Western) with him in the White House one evening, which we thoroughly enjoyed. He showed us love and consideration, and it was the experience of a lifetime. After our return home we received a handwritten letter from Uncle Harry. He said:

> Your visit was all too short as far as I was concerned. If you enjoyed your stay here I am very happy. It was a lonesome place after you left. Everyone—doormen, butlers, maids, and valets—thought you were quite the nicest family to visit here ever. So did your old uncle. If you had a good time I am happy.

Introduction

I have this letter today, and it is one of my treasures. Later, when we were back home visiting my grandparents' farm, Uncle Harry and Aunt Bess were also there. My mother was telling Uncle Harry how wonderful our stay was in the White House. She said that there was only one complaint, and that was from her youngest, the five-year-old. She was not able to run into the kitchen and get her crackers that she was accustomed to having throughout the day. Uncle Harry laughed and said, "Well, if I had known that, she could have had a whole box of crackers." I also had the unique experience of spending three summers working at the Truman Library when I was in high school. I helped Rose Conway with whatever project she needed me to do. Life was good!

Summer visit at the White House with Uncle Harry. Mary (left) and her family.

Uncle Harry and Aunt Bess arriving in Independence on January 21, 1953 upon returning to private life. Mary is on the right side of the picture at her Uncle Harry's left (circled). (Photo courtesy of UPI)

Mary as a teenager with Uncle Harry
(Photo courtesy of University of Saint Mary)

PART I

HOPELESSNESS FOLLOWED BY SUPERNATURAL HEALING

CHAPTER 1

THE BEGINNING OF MISERY

I am a walking miracle! I know many do not know of the faith message concerning healing, but I am alive today because of it. I was dying with an incurable disease that no doctor could heal. I got a hold of the truth of the Word of God about healing and it saved my life. My life was filled with many years of misery and hopelessness and then God, in His kindness, mercy, and love, pursued and rescued me. I like to say that He thundered from heaven when He heard my cry. Believing and confessing His Word brought wholeness, healing, and victory into my life! This is a truth that cannot be denied. I am a living testimony to this truth.

When I was in my thirties I decided to take oil painting classes. I had always loved art and decided the time was right, since my children were in school all day. I loved it from the very beginning. I was painting colorful landscapes and snow scenes. My teacher thought I was good and was very encouraging to me. My family liked my work and, after a few years, I was pleased at some of the results and happily gave each family member one of my paintings. During this time I began to have strange headaches, dizzy spells, and odd sick feelings. The doctors were puzzled about what was wrong with me. This went on for a few years, and it was frightening not knowing what was wrong. We thought it might be some kind of allergy, but to what we did not know. After checking out a few things with no results, my husband, Joe, suggested I give up painting for just one month. He thought maybe I was affected by the solvents in the oil paint. I was appalled at the idea. How could I give up painting? Surely, that was not the problem. But as time went on, and I was sick more and more, I finally agreed to stop for a month to see if there would be any change. I was heartsick to discover the oil paints were indeed the source of my problem. My symptoms and dizziness went away when I stopped breathing the paints and varnishes. I was glad to be well. I felt better than I had felt in several years. I had no dizzy spells. Knowing that I could not go back to painting was a real heartache and disappointment for me. The Scriptures say that the devil comes to steal, kill, and destroy. (See John 10:10.) Painting was the first of many things that were taken from me.

During this time I also developed allergies to anesthetics, antibiotics, and other medications. I was also becoming more and more sensitive to cigarette smoke. Unfortunately, most of my brothers and sisters smoked at that time. As my allergies became worse, family gatherings became very difficult for me. I suffered through many of these smoky functions for years. During one of these times, my parents' family room was so full of smoke that I could not breathe. Everyone was talking, laughing, and enjoying each other as I moved to the hall and sat on the floor, looking in. I was still breathing the smoke, but since I was not really a part of the conversation anymore, only peering in from the hall, I decided to go home. As Joe and I left, I told my mother I would not be able to come to family functions anymore because the smoke made me too ill. After I left, my father decided that from now on the ones who wanted to smoke (which was the majority) were relegated to the basement. No more smoking in the house! That is the way it was for years. I was so grateful for my parents' love and consideration. My family obliged without complaint.

Our Life Changes

Joe and I had built a large, split-level home on three-fourths of an acre in Independence, Missouri, about ten minutes from both of our parents. That is where we raised our children—a beautiful daughter, Terri, and a wonderful son, Paul. In the spring of 1985 I decided to wallpaper the recreation room where my children played. It was a big undertaking since it included a large stairwell with high ceilings. It took me many long days to complete it. My body was so sore from climbing up and down the ladder, reaching, bending, stooping, and stretching. These were things I was not used to doing. The evening that I finished I felt a funny sensation in my lower back. The next day excruciating nerve pain set in through my back, hip, and down my leg. The pain was so bad I could not even lie on the bed or sit in a chair. I spent three days on my back on the carpeted floor. Realizing I was not getting any better, I went to my doctor, who hospitalized me. Test results showed a herniated disc and three bulging discs in my lower back. The doctor said I could go home, but ordered me to bed for three months. My mother immediately called her church friends, and they started praying for me.

I was in and out of bed for a year. The pain was so unbearable I could not move. I could only lie in one position, and that was flat on my back. I could not sit or walk or the pain would be even worse. I definitely could not do steps. Because the kitchen was downstairs, I was trapped upstairs in the bedroom. Joe put a mini refrigerator in the guest bedroom so I could get something to eat while he was at work. It was a nightmare! Because of my allergies to medication I could not take anything to relieve my pain. The physical therapy program at the hospital did not help me, and I could not have surgery because I was allergic to anesthetics. There seemed to be no answer.

A Helping Hand From Joe

The pain was so bad that I could not do anything for myself. I could only stand in the shower briefly, so washing my hair was a problem. One day Joe decided he would help me out with this. He had me lay with my head at the foot of the bed. He got the old plastic baby tub from the basement and filled it with water, putting it on a chair at the foot of the bed. He then proceeded to wash my hair. While he was soaping my hair, the old tub split open and all the water ran over the mattress, soaking into the carpet. Joe was upset, and I was lying there feeling helpless. I hated every day that I was so dependent and all the trouble and work I was causing. We never tried that again!

The Beginning of Misery

Struggling in Pain

I struggled with pain on and off for four years. At some point during that first year, I was finally able to get out of bed, but I could not sit long at all.

I could not drive, it was too painful. If I dared go out anywhere to visit or go to a restaurant, I would have to get up every few minutes and walk around. I could not ride in the front seat of the car, so I had to lie down in the back seat. I could not sit on anything soft, so Joe cut some boards that I sat on (on top of the sofa) when we visited people. Not comfortable, but bearable. If we encountered stairs with no elevator, Joe would carry me up! This was not an easy task. We got some strange looks, and I usually felt embarrassed, but Joe did not. We eventually installed an elevator chair in our home when we realized I had not healed sufficiently to climb stairs. We finally decided we would have to move to a one-level ranch house. Our present house was just too difficult for me to get around. We had built this house, loved it, and had raised our children in it for fifteen years. It was the only home we had ever owned. My father always had a garden in our backyard, and he never did anything in a small way. One summer evening I picked 300 tomatoes! We had many wonderful memories, so this was a difficult decision to make. I knew Joe loved this home and how hard it was for him to move, but he did what he had to do.

CHAPTER 2

MOVING AND COPING

In 1986 we moved from our home in Independence across the Kansas City metro area, about thirty minutes away, to an area with many lovely, old ranch homes. Beautiful thirty-year-old oak trees lined the streets. Large yards proliferated in our neighborhood, and our location was convenient to everything. Every morning I got up early and walked those streets to strengthen my back. Eventually, I improved enough to drive on short errands and was finally out of the horrible, constant pain, but I had to be so careful. I still could not bend, lift, or move my body in a natural way, and there was so much I could not do. If I went to the grocery store by myself it took a lot of time and effort. I would have a store employee put the heavy sacks in my car. When I got home it was a long process of unloading cans and other items two at a time and sliding them on the kitchen floor from the garage. Once I got everything on the kitchen floor, I would have to kneel as I took each thing and brought it up to the counter. Bending over to get something off of the floor was totally out of the question. Finally I would grab hold of the counter top and pull myself up without bending my back. Standing, I now could put things away in the cabinets and refrigerator.

Joe had also fixed a small ramp for me to walk over the two deep steps that went to the garage from the kitchen. That is where our washer and dryer were located, so I was able to do the laundry again. I also was glad to be able to cook again and take care of many things that I used to consider mundane chores. I was determined to do everything that I possibly could so Joe could relax when he got home from work.

Could It Get Harder?

I had been in a car wreck years before all my back problems surfaced.

Moving and Coping

A truck crashed into the back of my car while I was stopped for a red light. I watched in the rear view mirror as he came speeding towards me. He had his head turned talking to the passenger and never turned back to see where he was going. If I had moved the car I would have been in oncoming traffic, so I just laid on my horn and hoped and watched with dread as he plowed into the rear of my car. It did not occur to me in those days to pray at such times. He crashed into me with such force that I had a bad whiplash, causing the discs in my neck to be weakened.

After our move, the unthinkable happened. The two weakened discs in my neck bulged out of place when I sneezed. This was even worse than the back problem, since it affected my whole body. I now had severe nerve pain and numbness down my arms, and in my back, hips, and down my legs. I could not move my head left or right, or look up or down. I was in another nightmare and despair set in. I had to wear a neck brace, and, of course, driving was out of the question again. I had to put pillows all around my head at night so I would not move in my sleep and set off incredible nerve pain. I would stand in the shower crying and begging God to work a miracle. One day, in terrible pain, I stood in my kitchen looking out the window. I looked up toward heaven, the best I could, and cried out to God. I made Him a personal promise—if He would give me a miracle. Of course, I had no faith for this and did not even know if He really heard me. God seemed so far away. I hoped for a miracle, but did not really expect one. I did not know anyone who had gotten a miracle! I was so desperate and tired of the pain. I felt like an incredible burden, and I was back to merely existing again.

Trying to Become Whole

More time passed, and I slowly improved. However, I still was not able to walk up and down steps. I decided I was going to conquer this at last. As recommended therapy, I started slowly walking up and down my basement steps. This was more than my back could tolerate. It caused the disc to shift against the nerve again. A few days later I was bedridden—again. I lost all the progress I had made the last couple of years. My daughter, Terri, worked a few blocks from home, so she gave up her lunch hour during this time to hurry over and fix my lunch. I was very grateful, as I knew this was an imposition. Joe was upset at the thought of repeating what we had gone through when this first happened to me. He told me in a very firm tone that he was not going to do this again. He just couldn't. He strongly urged me to get surgery. I did not blame him for feeling this way. I did not know how I was going to cope with it myself. At the same time, I was shocked that he said this to me. Didn't he know that the surgery would probably kill me? We had discussed this many times. Panic and more despair set in. My mind was spinning. How could I get surgery with my allergy to anesthetics and antibiotics? I desperately wished I could run away and hide somewhere. I did not care where it was as long as it was away from everyone who had to deal with me. I was a burden again and very frightened. At that moment I felt my support fade away. How was I going to climb out of this horrible pit?

Paul Graduates in New York

I did not have the surgery because of my allergies. We just coped the best we could. As time went on I was finally able to get out of bed again, but sitting for any length of time became impossible again. When my son, Paul, graduated from Cornell University in Ithaca, New York, in 1989, I was determined to attend his graduation ceremonies in spite of my problems. I still could not climb stairs. I also knew I could not fly because I could not sit that long. So Joe built a bed in the back of our van. Joe had to do all the driving for the three-day trip. I suffered the entire way. I felt every little bump in the road in my neck with nerve pain traveling all down my body. It was excruciating, but I managed to keep most of it to myself. I did not want to complain or have Joe listen to me moan through the whole trip. As difficult as it was, I was glad I went. It meant so much to Paul that we were there. Paul had been awarded twelve college scholarship offers upon his graduation from high school. The fact that he was accepted into this prestigious university made us all proud. The graduation was wonderful, and we were your typical proud parents. As we left a parking lot one dark night, Joe accidentally backed into a pole. It was the one time I had decided to sit up front instead of lying down in the back, because it was a short distance to our hotel. The force of the hit jerked my neck again with all the severe, sickening, nerve pain flooding back. The pain lasted for hours. Why did everything that could go wrong, always go wrong? We definitely were not under the blessings the Bible talks about. Why did everything always happen to us—to me? We spoke about the black cloud that we felt was hovering over us.

Joe helped Paul finish packing, and we left for home. At one point I was in so much pain that when Joe and Paul spotted a Sears store they went in and bought an air mattress. We thought this might cushion me from the jolts on the highway. This stop took a lot of time, as Joe and Paul took turns blowing up the mattress. They placed it on top of my firm mattress, and we were ready to travel again. It was only a few minutes before I knew that this was not going to work. With each little movement of the van I would roll back and forth on top of the air mattress. This was even more painful. I got my courage up to tell them to stop the car. They had to undo all they had just done. At least Joe was always willing to try something different to help me, even though it usually failed.

On the last night at the motel someone broke into the van and stole our camera with all the special graduation pictures we had taken. This was the only night that Joe had hidden our camera in the car. That black cloud again! The pictures were irreplaceable. I knew Paul had to be very disappointed, but he never uttered one word of complaint. He was extremely sensitive and kind.

CHAPTER 3

THE DAY GOD INVADED

In early 1985 we got the news that my father had prostate cancer. The oncologist determined that chemotherapy would do nothing for this type of cancer, but suggested surgery plus hormone treatment. My father agreed to the surgery, but before he would commit to the drug treatment, I took him to Memorial Sloan Kettering Hospital in New York for a second opinion. He was in a weakened condition after the surgery, but we knew he had to go immediately. Since I was the only one available, and it was before all my back problems, I flew with my mother and dad to New York, and I took care of everything. I had always dreamed of seeing New York, but not like this. It was a difficult trip with my dad's weakness, but I managed to get him to the hospital the next day. We were disappointed that they had nothing different to offer him. Even though my father had an administrative job most of his life, he was a physically strong man. He had grown up on a farm and was still quite active. The doctor remarked how healthy my dad was after his examination. Dad snapped back, "That's what the other doctors have said to me, but I have cancer, don't I?" We flew back home, and he started the recommended treatment. He lived for five more years. I was very close to my father, and he relied on me to keep track of all his medical records. He conferred with me about his treatments, as he did with his other children.

In the spring of 1989 my father was hospitalized after the cancer had spread to his bones, and he developed a cancerous brain tumor. Radiation treatment temporarily reduced the tumor, but the doctors felt it was only a matter of time. Even though we prayed for our father, we never thought to turn to God for healing. All my father wanted to do was go home. So, knowing he did not have much longer to live, we took him home. My seventy-three-year-old mother bore the burden of his care for a while. Eventually, even with hospice visiting, it became too much for her. After a month or so my brother, sisters, and I took turns helping out. As time went on, and we knew death was near, we all moved into our parents' house and lived together the last two weeks of my dad's life. He spent most of his time in a hospital bed in the large, first floor family room where his recliner used to be. My father never complained or demanded. He graciously complied with whatever we told him he needed to do. He was remarkable! We would have done anything for our dad. We loved and respected him so much. The last two weeks of his life were excruciating to watch. He was in constant, horrible pain. I had never watched anyone die before. When Joe asked my father if he was in pain one day, he quietly remarked, "Only when I move."

Prayers Answered After Fifty Years

My father was raised in a Christian home and believed in God. After he married my mother, he went to Mass every Sunday, even though he was not Catholic. He sent his children to Catholic schools and taught them their catechism, a summary of the church's doctrine. My mother had been praying for almost fifty years that my father would become Catholic. While he was in the hospital for radiation treatments, he had a vision that greatly affected him. After that he decided to join the Catholic Church.

My mother quickly arranged for the pastor to visit Dad at home on the day he returned from the hospital. My sister, Rita, was the only one of his children who was there. My mother was excited as she and Rita rushed around preparing for the pastor's arrival. To my mother's great joy, Dad was accepted into the Catholic Church after all those years. The pastor's remark to my mother when he left the room was that this was an unusually good man. After Joe got home from work he drove me to Independence. As I walked into the room I joked with my dad and said, "Who says God doesn't answer prayers. It only took fifty years for this one!" He just smiled. My father was a believer and a good man who kept the commandments and lived a Christian life. I feel that this blessing was mainly for my mother, who had faithfully asked God for this for fifty years. Because of her faith and persistent prayers, God gave her this desire of her heart.

In and Out of the Earthly Realm

As death neared, my dad had some unusual experiences. He seemed to be drifting in and out of the earthly realm. He managed the strength to tell us he loved us. He tried to explain what he was experiencing, but he was never able to find the right words. We just knew something remarkable was happening.

Two days before his death my father tried to communicate something he considered very important, but because of his weakened condition he could barely talk. My mother had spent thirty minutes trying unsuccessfully to understand what he wanted to say. One by one all nine family members who were in the house drifted into the room and surrounded his bed. He seemed to be strengthened by the presence of his family, and for a few minutes, his speech became stronger.

Dad spoke of a circle and held up his watch, pointing to its face. He felt like he was in a circle and that it was important for him to stay there, but he could not clarify it any further. He also said that every time he woke up he felt like he had been in a long battle and his legs were all bruised. He said this even though he knew he had not been out of bed. A few days later, at his death, we noticed his legs, previously white, were heavily bruised and blackened.

God Invades

On Saturday, before noon, two days before my father's death, my mother left to meet her cousin for lunch. Eight of us were still in the house. We were all in the family room with my father, but one by one we all strolled out of the room to attend to other things, except for Rita. She was sitting in a recliner facing my father's bed. Rita said later that she "knew" she was going to be alone in the room with Dad. Once she

20

was alone, things began to happen. Short, repetitive phrases (prayers) came to Rita's mind in rapid succession. Then God started giving Rita "prophetic messages" for three of us in the family. One of the messages He told her concerned me. He said, *"Mary will be well."* She said everything got completely black! She thought she was going to die. Rita then prayed, "Dear God I don't want to die." It was difficult to judge time, but she believed it was just a few minutes. A distant light appeared in the middle of the darkness. Her head was jerked toward the window side of the room, and she was transfixed toward the midday sun. For a moment she could not move. There was tremendous sunlight streaming through the window shining in on our father, who was lying in the hospital bed a few feet from the window. The room and window faced north, and there was no way that this kind of heavy beam of sunlight could have naturally shown in that window at that time of day. Rita was joyous to be alive! She was happy that God had given her encouraging messages for some of her family.

This was a new and surprising experience for her, but she knew she had heard from God. At that time, we knew nothing about prophecy. We had no exposure to it at all and no one to ask, even though it is discussed clearly in 1 Corinthians, chapters twelve and fourteen. Later that day, Rita called everyone back into the room. Joe helped gather the family, telling them that Rita had experienced a vision and received some messages.

No one knew what to think about what Rita was saying. We had never heard anything like this before. Some believed her, and others thought she had some kind of psychotic breakdown, even though they admitted she seemed perfectly normal. It was such a powerful encounter that Rita had no doubt that she had heard from God. It did not matter about some of the others' skepticism. She knew it was God and has never wavered from that belief or the truth of the prophetic messages!

A Sovereign Deliverance

Rita was now sitting on a stool next to the head of Dad's bed. He was sleeping. I was sitting on a barstool on the other side of the bed holding my father's hand. Suddenly my hand started to shake and tremble, and the trembling traveled up my arm to my shoulders and into my body. As it traveled up my arm and into my body it became stronger and stronger. I did not know what was happening, except it felt like a tornado inside me. The force inside me was incredible—very powerful. What was going on? My whole body vibrated and shook. I was afraid and began to cry softly. It seemed like it would go on forever, but it was only a few minutes. Joe stepped up to keep me from falling off the barstool, and then my head went uncontrollably back. I let out this long, strange cry from deep within. Then it was over, and my body was at peace. Everyone in the room was staring at me in silence. I felt embarrassed and not a little ridiculous. To say I was confused was an understatement. Everyone in the house at the time witnessed this. I did not have any idea what had happened to me. I only knew it was very unpleasant. Rita, on the other hand, was glowing and happy. She was enthralled and captivated that she had heard from God in such a powerful way. Even though she was somewhat mystified and unsettled by this, and did not know what it meant for her life, she was happy to have heard from God.

Understanding Comes Seven Years Later

It would be seven years before I knew that the all-powerful, loving God had sovereignly delivered me of an evil spirit at my father's bedside. I have no doubt, now, that it was a deliverance. I have seen many since then in healing prayer ministry. I believe God freed me from a spirit of fear of death (2 Tim. 1:7; Heb. 2:15). I am convinced of this because there was such a difference in me after this incident. I had struggled for many years with an unusual and abnormal fear of death. Many nights I would lie awake thinking about it. I could not seem to help it. The thought of death was extremely frightening to me. I do not remember the origin of the fear. I just know that the Lord, in His mercy and love, set me free from a spirit of fear surrounding death. Since then I have had no such fear. I am amazed that the Lord did this sovereignly, without my even asking, or knowing to ask, or even knowing at the time what had happened. What a good and merciful God we serve!

As I thought about the unusual blessings God granted to Rita and me at my father's bedside, I came to believe that it might have sprung from two circumstances. First, my father was an unusually righteous man, and God gives abundant blessings to such a man and his descendants (Ex. 20:5–6; Deut. 5:9–10, 28:1–14; 30:1–10). Second, his sons and daughters had shown him extraordinary care, honor, and respect. God has made it clear in the Scriptures how important is His commandment to honor your parents (Ex. 20:12; Deut. 5:16; Eph. 6:2). Whatever the reason, I know God sovereignly intervened in our lives that day, and I am thankful for it.

CHAPTER 4

HOPE BEFORE MORE SUFFERING

Finally, the Right Help

When my father was in the hospital for his radiation treatments in 1989, my sister, Rita, took it upon herself to ask his neurologist for a recommendation for a new doctor for me. This was during the time of a relapse into more back problems, and I was in and out of bed. I still could not stand or sit for any length of time.

Joe went with me to the new doctor. I told him about my neck and back problems. He grabbed my head and started roughly rolling it around. When I objected and said he was hurting me, he gruffly said he had to examine me and continued. His actions moved the discs around, and the nerve pain started in immediately. After he had done his damage he told me he would not do surgery on me because of my allergies. It would be too dangerous. He then asked me, "Well, what do you want from me?" I told him I could not go on like this, and asked if there was something he could do for me. He asked again, "What do you want from me? I'm a surgeon. There is nothing I can do!" I tried to hold back my tears and began to plead with him. Surely there was something someone could do for me. He hesitated for a moment then asked us to wait as he left the examination room and went to his office. When he returned he handed me the name of a clinic and said he had heard good things about it. Some of the baseball players from the Kansas City Royals had been treated there. He did not know enough about it to recommend it, but it seemed worth a try. We thanked him and left. If I had not persisted, I would not have obtained this information.

I went to The Back Center in Overland Park, Kansas. As Joe and I approached the door we were surprised that there was a full flight of steps and no elevator. We immediately concluded that the people here must not know what they were doing. How wrong we were. Joe investigated and found another entrance with no steps. I had to lie down for my consultation, because I was still not able to sit very long. After my examination, I was told that I had lost most of my muscle mass and that this was very dangerous. I was in very bad shape. Of course, we already knew that!

Ed, the therapist, a kind and knowledgeable man, told me he could help me. He said if I could hang in and do these treatments that "they would hurt me, but they would not harm me." Oh great, more pain to look forward to! I was told that the first two weeks would be the worst, and that many people dropped out during this time. I told him I would *not* be one of those people.

Hit Again

Not long after starting therapy my car was hit from behind again as I sat at a stoplight. The familiar nerve pain started in again from my neck and back. When would all of these horrible incidents end? I made it through all of the painful physical therapy and weight lifting. It was a lot of work, but I gradually started to improve. The pain started to diminish, and strength returned to my body. They had devised a special program for back problems and it was effective. Eventually, I was well enough to continue my therapy at home. I spent an hour each morning doing exercises before I started my day. This was necessary for me to be pain free. Anytime I skipped a few days the pain would return, so I faithfully did the physical therapy every day for many years. I still could not walk up steps or lift heavy objects, but now I could walk, sit, and drive free from pain. It was a miracle! I had started this treatment before my father came home from the hospital. I was happy he knew I was finally on the road to recovery. If it had not been for this new therapy, I would not have been able to spend time with my dad during his last few months. I later wrote the neurosurgeon and urged him to recommend this place to some of his other patients. I told him that this therapy worked when nothing else did. I thanked him for sending me to The Back Center. I hoped that my letter would encourage the doctor to recommend this clinic to some other desperate person. Even though my situation was much improved, and I was out of constant pain, I was bound to daily physical therapy just to maintain a degree of normalcy.

Mystery Illness

In September, more than three years after our move from Independence, I began having strange headaches, dizziness, and nausea again. I did not know what was wrong. The nights seemed to be the worst, and I would leave my bed and go to the family room sofa, where I got a little relief. I could not understand it. This went on for months. I began to realize that I felt better when I left my house for a few hours and upon returning I would get sick. We were puzzled again. We looked into every possible reason. We even hired an environmental engineer to come check out our house for any gasses or poison. He informed us that his measuring devices were not sensitive enough to pick up what was causing my problem. He said that his equipment was not nearly as sensitive as the human nose in detecting trace levels of possible contaminants. We needed answers, but did not get any that day.

Because I was suffering so much, I decided to stay with my mother for a few days to see if a change of environment would improve my condition. After a few days with her I was feeling much better. We had never heard of environmental allergies and did not know what we were dealing with. I continued to have headaches, nausea, and dizziness every time I tried to stay in our house. We eventually decided we had to sell our home, even though we did not know what was wrong with it. I was never able to live in our house again. Each time I tried I became terribly ill.

A family member offered to let us live temporarily with her. We stayed in her guestroom on weekdays, but usually traveled to Independence to stay with my mother on weekends. After about a month we felt we had imposed on the family long enough. We moved in with my mother full time while we continued to search for a home

Hope Before More Suffering

I could live in. My mother spent many hours driving me back and forth to house hunt. We wasted a lot of time looking at new houses that made me sick with all my usual symptoms. We still did not know why.

Ultimately, we discovered a correlation between my sickness and the new insulation Joe had been putting in the attic. He had been installing it after work and on the weekends, starting over the master bedroom. My symptoms began about the same time Joe started that project. Formaldehyde from the new insulation had permeated the whole house. Since our house had not sold yet, Joe helped me up the ladder to the attic to check it out. The fumes from the new insulation made my stomach churn. It was clearly the source of the problem. Joe spent many hours removing the insulation that he had painstakingly installed, but it did not help. The house and furniture were already saturated with chemicals. New insulation was also part of the reason why I had problems in the new houses we were shown. After this discovery we did not look at any house younger than ten years. This period of time gave the insulation and other new materials time to "outgas," or clear of chemicals. The more information and contacts we made with people with this problem, the more we realized how few our options were. Avoidance seemed the only solution.

Surgery the Hard Way

That first summer after we had moved in with my mother and after a routine mammogram, I was told I would need surgery to remove two growths in my breast. The doctor was hopeful that it was not serious, but this was very stressful, on top of everything else. I could not dwell on the fact that I might have cancer. My main concern was surviving the surgery. With my allergies to antibiotics and anesthetics, how was I going to do this? The doctor told me it could be done as an outpatient procedure. I really pressed him to use a local anesthetic, which he did not prefer. He finally agreed. I asked him to use half of the usual amount of anesthetic because of my sensitivity. It was obvious he was anxious about this, but he reluctantly agreed. All my attention was focused on surviving the surgery and not on the results they might find.

I took a little tape recorder as a distraction to help block out the surgery. As the doctor gave me the small amount of anesthetic that I had insisted on, he said: "Mary, I am putting the rest of this over here on the table. If at any time you want more, just say so and I will give you more." I nodded, knowing I would not ask for more.

This was the most difficult medical procedure I have ever had. I could faintly feel the incision and most of the surgery. It was not too bad in the beginning, but, as time passed, the anesthetic began to wear off, and I began to feel more pain. I reacted mildly a few times, and I knew the doctor wanted to give me more anesthetic, but I refused to even consider it. The thought of how sick it would make me kept me from asking for it. I thought if I could just hang on a little longer it would be over. By the time they were through, I was completely drained and exhausted. The trauma, stress, and pain really took a toll. I was very ill for days from the amount of anesthetic that I did have. As I waited for the biopsy results, the realization of what they might find finally came over me. I was very relieved when I learned that the growths were benign. My family had been praying for me like they always did. Even though I prayed, I did not understand the power of prayer at this point in my life. I turned mainly to doctors and "works of man" even though I had lost all trust in them through a number of bad experiences.

One of the experiences involved treatment for the herniated disc in my lower back before I discovered The Back Center. I went to the hospital outpatient center for an epidural cortisone shot into my spine to block pain. I had resisted doing this, but the pain had become so constant and intense that I finally agreed. The doctor who handled the procedure accidentally put the needle into my spinal fluid and the drugs immediately shot up into my brain. I felt like my head would explode, and excruciating pain immediately set in. I became deathly ill. As I was lying there in fear and pain and unable to move, the nurse asked me if I would like to make my appointment for my second shot! I was stunned! I shook my throbbing head no, and it took great effort to keep from telling her that they were crazy if they thought I was coming back for more malpractice! I just wanted to get out of there as fast as I could. Of course, I knew I would never go back.

Another horrible incident happened at the same hospital. I was having so much esophageal pain, resulting from stress, that the doctor decided to insert a scope down my throat to examine the area. I asked if I needed an anesthetic for this, and he said I did even though I explained my sensitivity. With difficulty and after a number of tries, the nurse inserted a needle into my left arm. Soon I noticed my arm starting to swell as the anesthetic dripped in. She had accidentally put the needle into the muscle instead of the vein. The doctor became extremely agitated and started yelling at the team when I pointed it out to them. He jerked the needle out and went around to my other arm. The doctor himself placed a needle for the Valium IV into my hand. Later I developed blood clots in that arm. The *Physicians' Desk Reference* clearly states that Valium should *never* be put into the hand, that it causes blood clots! I also found out later that I could have had the procedure without an anesthetic. After these incidents I avoided doctors if it was at all possible. If I absolutely had to get medical attention it caused me great anxiety.

CHAPTER 5

TRAGEDY STRIKES

The summer of 1990, when we moved in with my mother, we asked our son, Paul, to continue living at our house until it sold. He agreed even though he did not want to. Paul was twenty-three, and it had been almost a year since his graduation from Cornell University. He was working for Sprint Corporation as a computer engineer. I felt it was a miracle that he was back home. All of his friends and contacts were in the eastern United States, so when he got a good job here, I was incredibly happy.

Paul had always been a special child. When he was barely three years old he climbed up to my grandmother's old upright piano and began to play *Alley Cat* by ear. He took piano lessons for many years, eventually composing his own pieces and winning many trophies in music contests. He was very talented in many areas and also became a computer expert. People were drawn to him, and he had many friends. Paul was gentle, kind, and charitable. He encouraged and helped anyone in need. That included giving away his hard earned money without a thought of it being repaid. He was a live spark in our little family of four. He and his older sister, Terri, a very special person in her own right, were very close.

New Sports Car

Paul had decided to trade in his late model sedan for a new, black Ford Probe sports car. His father and I were opposed to that because of the financial loss he would take on the car he had just recently bought. I also had other concerns. Paul was six feet five inches tall, one inch taller than his father, and had absolutely no headroom in that little car. He had to position the seat very far back to be able to fit, and he had to drive in that position. I felt he was not safe and expressed that to him. He just smiled and said it was what he wanted, and that it would be all right. I knew he was determined to do this, so I finally gave up saying any more.

That whole summer, whenever I saw Paul in his black Probe, I got a very uncomfortable feeling. It was a feeling of doom, a heaviness. I did not understand it, but whenever I saw him and the car together, this heaviness would come over me. One day he invited me to ride home with him from church. He wanted me to drive his car, so I took the keys and smiled in spite of the sad feeling that was sweeping over me. As I drove the five blocks home, with Joe following in our car, Paul was bubbling over with excitement showing me all the little extras in his beloved car. The feeling inside me was so overwhelming that I could not help gently expressing again my concerns about the lack of headroom and his safety in this car. He explained how it had anti-lock brakes, that nothing bad could possibly happen, and that I had no reason to worry. The whole time I was in the car with him, the same uncomfortable heaviness and sadness persisted, and I could not shake it. Then, after he drove home, the feeling would lift. I did not understand what was going on with me, so I never talked about this to anyone. I was so wrapped up in my own troubles that I did not really focus on this, something I would regret later. I was too busy trying to survive.

Paul's Deadly Accident

On the morning of September 29, 1990, after we were living with my mother for a few months, we lost Paul in a horrible automobile accident. He was traveling to St. Louis to visit a new friend. Paul was driving much too fast and lost control of his car. He went off the road into a field, and as he hit a barbed wire fence, the car rolled over nine times. Then it burst into flames.

That afternoon, when the doorbell rang, I looked out and saw two policemen standing on the porch, and that heaviness came over me again. I thought, "It's time. This is it." I knew something bad had happened to

Paul. I started asking them immediately about him. They would not answer any of my questions until I sat down. I was hoping he was lying in a hospital somewhere, but when the officers said he was dead it was all I could do to keep breathing. I pressed them on how fast he was driving, and they did not want to tell me. I asked them if it was one hundred miles per hour? They nodded yes and said no more. We found out later that Paul had been driving one hundred twenty miles per hour. My reaction to learning this was immediate anger. I could not believe that he had been so irresponsible and careless with his life. We were told that he died of a massive brain injury. I went into deep shock. I felt like my insides had shattered and that my heart had been ripped out and crushed. I had never felt such incredible pain. I was very close to my son and did not know how I could live without him. This deep grief was an added burden to my body and spirit.

The news was devastating to our daughter, Terri, losing her only brother. It had always been just the two of them. My husband, for one brief moment, fantasized that maybe his car had been stolen, someone else was driving, and Paul was really safe somewhere.

Unspeakable Pain

I did not care about much anymore. I desperately wanted to get well, but I wallowed in my grief for years. I could not seem to help myself. How could I be happy without my son? I knew I could not. Life would never be the same for us. I felt my life was over. Music had always been a passion of mine. In the past, I did not think I could ever live without music—but now music would not be a part of my life. I just would not listen to it. I continually thought about Paul's last moments. In my mind I would get in the car with him. I could visualize him driving down the freeway. I would see his precious face and imagine how he felt as he lost control of the car and it started to roll over. What was running through his mind? Was he terrified? What kind of pain did he suffer? I even imagined him at the moment of death, his spirit leaving his body and soaring above the flaming wreck as he glanced back at it on his way to heaven. In my grief and shock my mind did all kinds of

Tragedy Strikes

strange things. I wondered if he knew the unspeakable pain we were in. As the years passed, sadness seeped deeply into my spirit. I had no joy at all. I knew my heart was broken beyond repair. I still prayed during this time, but, in spite of my prayers, I continued to get worse.

CHAPTER 6

THE AFTERMATH OF
PESTICIDE POISONING

Spraying in the Wind!

One spring day in April 1992, I was at the kitchen window watching as our neighbor sprayed his lawn with herbicide in a thirty-mile-per-hour wind. I wanted desperately to move my van as it was in the driveway right next to where he was spraying, but I knew I could not go outside. I could not imagine anyone spraying in these high winds. It was getting all over him as well. My mother was gone and Joe was at work, so I just stood there helplessly watching as my van got saturated. The next morning I woke up very ill, my allergies worse. I was even *more* sensitive to my environment. How could I be even worse? Because of the high winds, the herbicide had blown in an open kitchen window that faced his yard. This poisoning brought my allergies to a new level. Now I was sick in my mother's house, my only place to live. We called an out-of-town environmental doctor for help. There was no help! I was again desperate. This horrible pit was an all too familiar place to be. I had to wear a charcoal mask to breathe, and it was heavy and hot. The weight of it left huge painful marks on my nose and face. I hated it. I hated my life. I was so sick. The mask was so horribly uncomfortable I would go outside to breathe without it, looking for relief, and the car exhaust fumes would affect me. We were one block from a four-lane highway. I had to move to the tiny tiled foyer at the other end of the house, where there was no furniture or carpet. We closed the big oak doors. As I sat in this very small space looking out the glass front door, it was all too clear that my world was getting smaller and smaller.

The Aftermath of Pesticide Poisoning

Mother Cooperates

My mother was wonderful. She said yes to whatever I needed. She was in her own state of grief, as my father had died only eight months before we moved in with her. Joe approached her with the idea to remove the carpet from the hardwood floors in the part of the house we were living in. We felt this would remove a lot of the chemical residue. She immediately said yes. We asked my wonderful cousin, Linda, to come in and scrub every inch of the ten-room, two-story house—ceilings, walls, woodwork, cabinets, windows, everything. Finally, even after all of this work, there was only one room that I could use without the breathing mask. It was the kitchen. If I had to pick one room, I guess this was probably the best. At least I could cook and eat my food without wearing that awful mask. We put a sofa in there and kept the doors shut. I slept, ate, and lived there for two more years. I would lie awake at night and listen to the refrigerator cycle on and off. I was depressed and hopeless. I would look out the window and see life going on as usual, and I could not imagine being normal again. When I did venture out (without my mask) I used to think, as I passed people, that they probably thought I was just another normal person. I felt like an alien. I knew of no one with this problem that got well. Each had a horror story. Like me, they were just surviving. Some had moved to the desert or to mountaintops searching for clean air to breathe. Most had spent all their money trying to get well. Many had been deserted by their spouses. All lived in great fear and isolation.

Searching for Help in Texas

In 1993, a year after the pesticide poisoning, we decided to seek help at an environmental clinic in Texas. We learned of the clinic from the last doctor I spoke with. Joe drove me there and stayed for a few days to get me settled. We drove the five hundred miles in one day because I could not stay in a motel. At least I was able to help Joe drive on this trip.

35

We rented space in an apartment complex run by the clinic. The condominium had two bedrooms, a living room, and a small kitchen. The apartment was shared with one other person. This was difficult, since each person had different levels of environmental allergies.

When we arrived, my new roommate showed me my bedroom, and Joe proceeded to unload the car. By the time we got all of my things in the apartment my roommate was already sick. All of my things were making her ill. She told us we could not stay there. Joe and I just looked at each other. What were we going to do? I had an appointment in the morning with the head doctor at the clinic. I knew I could not stay in a hotel. Joe carried all our things back to the car. We were very tired from our trip, and the thought of getting back in the car was too much. Panic set in! Where would we go?

We were told about a place outside the city where people with environmental illnesses lived. We decided to drive out and take a look. As we pulled up to this deserted place, I got very anxious. I could not imagine staying there. They lived in tiny bare trailers with stainless steel walls, and the only furniture was a twin bed, a chair, and some metal wire shelves. The kitchen was across a field in a building by itself, with many stoves and refrigerators lining the walls. It was open with no doors, no heat, and no air-conditioning. The trailer park was so far from the clinic that driving back and forth numerous times a day on the freeway would be a problem. As we were being shown around, all I could think about was getting out of there. I could hardly hear what the sweet lady, who was giving us the tour, was saying. I just wanted to escape and escape immediately. My heart was pounding and I was pan-icky at the thought of having to stay there. The people looked very sickly and sad. As we looked around, we talked to a frail woman on oxygen who could hardly speak. Her voice was so weak. She told us how she had apparently shaken the symptoms of the disease at one time. However, she ignored all the doctor's advice and went to work for a lawn and garden nursery where they sprayed the trees and plants with insecticides. She also started refinishing furniture and used a lot of chemical paint strippers. Her health became worse than before, and

The Aftermath of Pesticide Poisoning

now she was dying. They were not going to be able to save her. Her condition really frightened me. I whispered to Joe that I could not stay there and could we please leave *now*.

When we got in the car Joe asked what we were going to do now. I told him to please take me back to the condominium. We had paid for it, and it was half mine. I suggested we leave everything in the car for now, so we would not make the other woman sick. This woman was going home in a few days, so we would just have to manage. When we returned, the woman had left, to stay with a friend for the night. She also decided she would go home a few days earlier than she had planned. All I could think of was, what if I had stayed at that depressing, difficult place in the country. The apartment we had reserved was now empty. She did come back the next morning and stayed for a few days until she was able to leave for home. Not having my things in there was a help to her, but inconvenient for us. We had to go to the car every time we needed something.

The apartments for the patients were sparse with no upholstered furniture or draperies. The floors were tile. The only furniture was a wrought iron table and chairs, a hard, wood bench with no cushions, and two twin beds in each bedroom with cotton mattresses. Ours actually sagged to the floor with a person on it, but not everyone had beds in this condition. Our mattresses had to be put on the floor to get any sleep at all. The first morning I walked out into the living area there were huge, Texas-size, long-legged spiders covering the walls, too many to count. With my heart pounding, I immediately got Joe. My roommate had been leaving boxes and trash on the tiny patio, and the spiders were nesting there and making their way into the apartment through the sliding glass doors. I wondered how she put up with this. We quickly started killing all the spiders, and Joe had to spend his limited time cleaning up her mess on the patio. Except for an occasional spider, that got rid of them, much to my relief. I was not comfortable sleeping with my mattress on the floor after that, but I had no choice.

We saw the doctor the next morning, and he explained all the treatments. I would have a sauna treatment every day, have many blood tests every week, have allergy tests, exercise, and eat only organic food on a rotation diet. Joe helped me find my way around to a few places before he had to leave for home. I took him to the airport, and I never felt so lonely as I did on my drive back to the clinic. The fear of the unknown and what was ahead of me was setting in. Joe and I had never been separated for more than a few days, and now we knew this could be for a very long time. Joe had no choice but to leave. Someone had to earn a living, and I certainly was not able to.

Sauna and Other Treatments

The sauna was the main treatment offered at the clinic. Seven or eight people, men and women together, wearing clean, cotton shorts and tee shirts would go into these huge, poplar wood saunas for thirty minutes or more. Their belief was that their program would benefit patients with a high chemical overload in their bodies. Many toxic chemicals are stored in the fatty tissues of the body. Their program of exercise, sauna, and massage therapy causes those chemicals to be released from the fatty tissue into the bloodstream and excreted. They said that the symptoms could temporarily be worse but that this would pass and improvement would be noted.

At the start of the program each day, vital signs were taken. Then niacin was given to each patient's tolerance. I could not take any niacin. Then patients would exercise for twenty minutes on bikes, treadmills, or rowers. Niacin was again given to the patient's tolerance, then into the sauna for thirty minutes. In the subsequent shower, you had to be in and out within five minutes and that included washing your hair. There were many people waiting, and there was only one shower, which was very surprising. Vital signs were taken again. Finally a massage was given for ten minutes. This was considered one session. The goal was three a day. I could only tolerate one session a day, and that took most of the morning. But I was determined to make this work.

The goal was to sweat out the chemicals that had built up in the fatty tissues. The smell inside the sauna from the chemicals coming from the sweaty bodies was far from pleasant. We were to refrain from eating onions and garlic while we were in the sauna program, and we quickly found out why this was encouraged! The talk in the sauna consisted of each person's horror story of how they got so sick, and any tidbits that might help someone else.

I was put on a four-day rotation diet. If I ate wheat on Monday I could not have it again until Friday. Each day I had to eat something different, and then not eat it again until the fifth day. I made up a chart and menu to help me remember what day I could have what food. This was also supposed to help unload the immune system so it could heal. Everything I did was time consuming and difficult, but I was now doing everything humanly possible to combat this disease. It was such a strange illness. I saw so much suffering and fear. I did not realize what a chemical world we live in until these allergies appeared.

After I had been at the clinic alone for almost three weeks, Rita flew in from Kansas City to spend some time with me. I was anxious to see her. It had been so hard. It was a forty-five minute drive to the airport in a very large, unfamiliar city. I was hoping I would not get lost, as I had only driven it once with Joe. I managed to pick her up without any trouble, but on the way back I made a wrong turn and it took us two hours to find our way back to the apartment.

Contaminated Condominium

My condominium was in a complex managed by the clinic, and patients were encouraged to stay there. One morning, four days after Rita had arrived, we returned to the condominium and discovered it was full of fumes. The noxious odor gave me a headache. I was so sensitive that I was not able to stay inside very long. Environmentally ill people are, of necessity, very careful about their living space. Panic sets in when the area is contaminated because there is no longer a safe haven.

Rita went upstairs to the condominium above mine which was being remodeled. The man doing the work turned out to be the son of the doctor that ran the clinic. Rita informed him that the fumes had filled my condominium and asked what they were going to do about it. He admitted to using "very foul stuff." He also said he knew the fumes had gone down an open vent to my condominium, because he did not seal the vent. Rita asked him if he would seal the vent immediately. He was reluctant because he was ready to paint. He said he had to paint now because they had a patient coming from the hospital that weekend. Rita asked him to stop. She told him the patient would be better off if they did not have to breathe fresh paint as every one of their patients had environmental allergies. The lack of compassion and understanding about environmental allergies surprised us.

He immediately called the woman who managed the condominiums and told her the problem. She told him to proceed and paint one room now and the rest when I was away for treatment. We tried to explain to him the fumes would still come into my condominium whether I was there or not when he painted. He told her that we had an emergency situation, that I was sick, and would she please come over and handle this problem. She would not come! Many hours later she returned my phone calls. I told her my condominium was contaminated, and that I would have to go home now in the middle of my treatments, and all the money I had spent was wasted. There was always a waiting list for the apartments, so there was no place else for me to stay. She was very insensitive to my needs. I convinced her to stop the painting until my husband could fly down and drive me home. Joe would come right away. I asked if I could borrow the air filtering machines that were in the empty apartment to help clean the air in mine. At first she refused, but, because I persisted, she finally gave her permission. I was amazed at her cold, heartless attitude toward me and toward some of the other patients. There had been complaints from others, but this was my first experience with her. Joe arrived the next morning and could smell the chemicals, so we packed the car and left for home.

I was glad to be out of the clinic situation but depressed at the thought of coming back to my one room. I was disappointed that there was so little progress from the three hard, expensive weeks in Texas. We decided to acquire our own sauna so I could do the treatments at home. It would be safer and much more economical. I was hopeful that

The Aftermath of Pesticide Poisoning

maybe this was the answer. A woman I met at the clinic said she had a sauna, and even though she was not well, using it had saved her life. I did my own sauna treatments five days a week for a number of years. I also ate as much organic food as I could find. I seemed to stabilize, but I never made much progress toward getting well. We wondered why I was not making dramatic improvements. I was very faithful and regular about doing everything I had learned at the clinic. I kept clinging to the notion that in time I would get better, but it just did not happen. We were still depending on doctors and our own methods.

More Back Problems

My back condition continued to make my life a challenge. I decided to sort through some things for my mother on the second floor of the house, but I was still unable to climb stairs in spite of my daily therapy. I had to crawl up one step at a time until I reached the second floor. After getting to the top and starting in on my project, I felt a second disc in my back herniate. There was no mistaking it. Nerve pain immediately shot down my leg. All the horror of being bedridden came flooding back. I managed to get downstairs by sitting on each step and lowering myself to the next step, holding the weight of my body with my arms. All the way down I was in such fear and anxiety. As I slowly descended the stairs, I decided I would not go to the doctor. Except for surgery there was nothing they could do for me, and surgery was not an option. I would handle this myself. I usually did my physical therapy once a day, first thing in the morning. Now I had to do the exercises continually, all day long. After three months of sleepless nights and painful therapy on my own, the pain left and strength returned. I was finally back to where I was before this happened and doing my exercise once a day again. Thank God I had these effective exercises from The Back Center.

CHAPTER 7

SUFFERING WITH ENVIRONMENTAL ILLNESS

For seven long years I struggled with environmental illness, also known as multiple chemical sensitivity. Because of the herbicide poisoning in 1992 my immune system rapidly declined. Eventually, I became allergic to nearly everything in my environment, including cigarette smoke, perfume, cleansers, detergents, lotions, fresh paint, car exhaust, pesticides, and almost anything new. I continued to develop many food and mold allergies. I was allergic to antibiotics, anesthetics, and most medicines, and eventually even vitamins.

My allergies became so severe that at times it was hard to leave the house. At my worst, I could not attend church, movies, or other events where there were very many people because of the prevalence of new clothes, perfume, and other chemicals. I could not go into shopping malls, theaters, office buildings, grocery stores, or even most people's homes, including those of my family. To breathe cleaner air, we had portable air filtering machines in our home, and I often had to wear that uncomfortable charcoal filtering mask when I ventured out. I was a prisoner in my home. The fear, pain, and isolation were unbearable.

I finally got my hopes up again when I discovered a doctor in the area who specialized in environmental medicine. He felt he could help me and started some new treatments. To our horror this good, caring man's treatments made my allergies even worse. He had started allergy testing, and because I was allergic to the glycerine in the solution, I developed equilibrium problems, nausea, ringing in the ears, and headaches.

We did not think things could get any worse but they did. I was so

42

Suffering With Environmental Illness

sensitive that I was now sick in the one room I had been able to live in. To stay in the house, I was back in the commercial mask, frightened and hopeless. I was always in the depths of hopelessness when bad things happened. I had nothing to cling to except my own feeble strategies for escape.

Due to my declining condition the doctor immediately prescribed three intravenous (IV) treatments to cleanse my liver from the overload of chemicals. Because I was now so sensitive, I could not even go inside his clinic for treatment like I had done before the allergy testing. I stayed outside in the car in the parking lot while a nurse wheeled the IV to the car. I was out in the cold parking lot for two hours thinking how unreal this all seemed. I was not able to finish the IV bag because my vein leaked and my arm and fingers became swollen.

The next morning I woke up with new symptoms. I was now sensitive to trees and pollen. The doctor assured me that these symptoms would clear with more IVs.

Three weeks later I took a second IV in the parking lot. I was grateful the doctor was willing to treat me in my car, but at the same time I seemed to get worse with each treatment. Eleven days later I took the third and last IV. I weighed 120 pounds at the start of the allergy treatments. My weight was now down to 104 pounds. After consulting long distance with another environmental doctor, it was decided that the IVs had overloaded my system. At that point, I could not tolerate *anything*. I was desperate!

The local doctor and his wife made a house call to inspect my living area. When he came in the house he quickly sensed from his own reactions that the home was full of old pesticide residues. He recommended that I get out of the house immediately. He felt it was imperative that I not spend another day in that house even though I was wearing a respirator.

No Place to Live!

I now had no place to live, so I had to move to my car. Joe took the back seats out of our van so I could at least lie down to sleep at night. It was

43

March and it was cold. I was in great despair! I could not help thinking about the homeless and that this was just a small taste of what they go through. I spent three cold, frightening weeks in my van. Fortunately, I had a cell phone so I could keep in contact with my family. The van was parked in the back driveway, and I would have to get out in the cold night for trips to the bathroom wearing my hat, coat, and gloves, hoping none of the neighbors saw me. They had no idea of the unusual activities going on in our house. If I could not sleep I would drive on the deserted night roads to my sister's house a half hour away and sit in her driveway for a while. It all seemed so strange. I was in my usual state of misery. Again, there seemed no way out.

Rescued From the Car

I finally was able to stay in the sunroom of a family member's house, only after the room was scrubbed and almost everything was removed. I lived there for a month. They did everything they could for me. They told me later that as they descended the stairs each morning they were afraid they would find me dead. They wanted to reach me before their child did. That is how sick I was and how bad I looked.

Eventually I ended up at my daughter's one bedroom apartment after much work on her part. I lived there for two years while Joe did everything he could think of to solve my problems. Joe was a Senior Staff Engineer at Allied Signal in Kansas City, with a master's degree in physics. Joe was used to solving difficult problems, but he could not solve this one no matter how hard he tried—and he tried on a daily basis for years. But nothing ever worked, and it always plunged us into deeper despair. We still felt like we were living under that black cloud, and we were! We were still trusting in ourselves and in our own devices. We were like the barren bush planted in the desert (Jer. 17:5–6).

During the time I was living with Terri, I was forced to listen to music again. I had no choice. It was her place, and she was going to listen to it. Terri loved music as much as I had. Slowly the joy of music returned as I unavoidably heard it each day. I began to take delight in it again.

Endless Searching for Help

I spent many hours reading and searching for help. My sister-in-law, Anthea, who lives in Colorado, spent many days on the telephone calling all over the United States seeking help for me. I tried every remedy of man, going to different doctors and consulting long distance with many experts. We heard about a researcher in another state who was experimenting with magnet therapy. I called him on two different occasions for consultations and information. He wanted me to be a part of his research and mailed me some information. His catalog showed magnets on everything you could imagine, from mattresses to hats, and all at very high prices. We could not believe a magnetic field would have any effect on pain or disease. I was thankful later that the cost was so high, because it kept me from wasting more money. At one point, to test this man's theory, Joe strapped a magnet on his back where he had pain and wore it for two days. He took it off when he realized his back pain was getting worse, not better. Desperation and ignorance cause people to do strange things, and we were definitely desperate.

I continued searching for man's answers to impossible problems. Each time I tried something new I would be filled with hope. I always believed I had at last found the answer and could get well, but it never happened. I continued to decline. I was preparing to die. I gave things away. Many times I begged God to save me not for my sake, but for my husband and daughter. I did not want them suffering through another premature death. It would be too much to bear.

Moth Ball House

After much searching we bought an older home, but I was never able to move in. The previous owners had saturated every closet, nook, and cranny with mothballs, and we were never able to get the smell out. Every time I entered the house it made me ill. Every night after work, Joe would do what was needed at that house. We bought an ozone generator that Joe would move from room to room until he had treated the whole house. He did this for weeks. Of course, it was risky for him to go in there night after night and breathe the residual ozone without risking damage to his lungs. But, he was determined to clean that house up so we would have a place of our own to live. After a year of remodeling and trying everything to clean it up enough for me to live there, we had no choice but to sell again. During all this time we were still living with my mother. Fortunately, because she had a huge two-story home, there was room for all of us. However, we had to put all our furniture in storage. Our things were in and out of storage for almost five years. This was another big expense. We continued house hunting, but there was always some reason why we could not buy a certain house because of my severe allergies. If previous owners installed new carpet, which most did to sell their home, or painted, treated for termites, added insulation, or used room deodorizer plug-ins and potpourri, then I could not move in.

Many people do not realize that plug-ins and spray deodorizers are man-made chemicals. They just mask odors; they do not remove the cause. I believe that no one should breathe these chemicals on a regular basis, particularly people with allergies or asthma.

A Foil Room: Another Bright Idea!

During this time we continued to call all over the country, talking to experts about environmental allergies. Companies sold all kinds of merchandise at big prices to help you survive. One company advised us to line a room with aluminum foil to block out external pesticides and chemicals. They told of someone who had done this successfully. We decided we had to try this. We bought a lot of expensive foil that is similar to aluminum foil, only heavier and thicker, and enlisted the help of family. Our family team spent many hours scrubbing and covering the ten-foot high ceiling and walls of my mother's kitchen and breakfast room where I would live and sleep. They were finally finished, and as Joe walked me in, with all the family watching who had worked so hard, my heart sank. I was allergic to the foil! I could not breathe in there! A heavy metallic smell filled the air, and I could feel it in my lungs. I was embarrassed and felt terrible about all the work everyone had done, and again, it was for nothing. I went back to Terri's small apartment in an even more hopeless state.

Joe was finally out of ideas. He said to me, "You are going to have to get better before you can get into another house." I knew he felt there was nothing more he could do. How could I get well? I knew Joe was finally through trying, so more despair set in. We still knew of no one with environmental illness who had completely recovered.

Buying Another Home

During all of this we were still house hunting. We finally bought a ranch style house about five minutes from Terri's apartment and close to my sisters' homes. Of course, I had allergic reactions in the house, so my moving in was not possible. We did have our furniture moved out of storage and into the house, and Joe spent time there. We hired the same movers, a family-run business and members of my mother's church, each time we needed to move our furniture. We hired them the first time to move our belongings across town from Independence. We hired them again when we had to sell that home and put everything back in storage. We hired them to move our things out of storage and into the "moth ball" house, which we owned a year and a half, but never lived in. We hired them again to take our furniture out of that house and put it back into storage. Later, when my mother decided to move to a retirement home, we had these same movers move our things into my mother's house in Independence. The last time we called them was to move our things from my mother's house to the last home we bought. They joked about how we must love to move. They had no idea about our problems.

Joe would bring me over in the evenings to this last house for short periods, for as long as I could stand it. He would play the piano, and for a brief time we would pretend that things were normal. Even though I did not feel good while I was there, I spent the time unpacking and hanging all the paintings I had done years earlier. I remember thinking that at least Joe would not have to worry about getting the house in order after I died. I would at least have done all of this for him. I felt so sad as I unpacked, put things away, and hung my paintings and family photographs knowing that I would never live there. I had a tremendous heartache over what I felt Joe was suffering and would suffer. I also knew my daughter, Terri, was fearful that I was going to die. It was a stress and fear we all lived with.

Going on a Macrobiotic Diet

I was constantly searching the natural world for healing. All the things I tried were man-made solutions. Among many other things, I had developed what is called a "leaky gut," which was contributing to my food allergies. It meant that I was not absorbing most of the nutrients from my foods. That is one reason why, no matter how much I ate, I remained skin and bones. I would eat two hearty plates full of food, and half an hour later I would be hungry again. I read how people had been healed from cancer on the macrobiotic diet and decided this might be my way out. Meat was not included on the diet, but fish and some things I had not eaten before were. Because I was so weak and hungry, I had to include fish at all three meals—a different type of fish at each meal. I ate seaweed, dandelion greens, and many exotic foods. Even though I disliked the diet, I was determined to make it work. As the weeks went by I started getting weaker and weaker. I was at the two-month mark when I became so weak I knew I was in trouble. I could not do the diet exactly as prescribed because of my food allergies. Joe said I needed to start eating meat again. My heart sank! Failure again! This diet had really been my last hope. I had tried everything I knew to try. If I could not do *this*, I had nothing else left. How could I get well? Due to my extreme weakness I started eating meat again the next day. Within two days I had some strength back. I felt that if I could have done the diet correctly, with all of the recommended foods, I would not have gotten weak, but that was not the case. But now what?

I had read some interesting and hopeful books by a famous environmental doctor who lived near the East Coast. I knew I was not able to make the trip there, but she offered thirty-minute phone consultations for $100 a call. In desperation, I called her four times. I was trying to do all the things she suggested, but on the fourth phone call, when she realized I was getting worse, not better, her tone changed significantly. She said she had nothing for me and that she was not my doctor. She suggested I go to the Texas clinic for help. I was panicked at the thought of going back to the clinic again. More money had been wasted with these phone consultations, and hope was dashed again.

Searching Again for Health in Texas

I traveled again to Texas to the environmental health clinic, the foremost clinic in the country for the treatment of environmental illness. After my experience the first time I did not want to go back, but I had nowhere else to turn. I stayed in a different condominium complex, which was not managed by the clinic. They were small, one bedroom apartments with privacy. Coming back really was the last thing for me to try. My height is 5' 9", and I weighed only one hundred four pounds. I was losing weight daily. At the time I did everything the doctors suggested, all the alternative medicine and treatments, which I would not now recommend. I just did not know any better. But, nothing helped. Or if it did the help was only temporary.

Sauna Treatments Again

I did the sauna treatments again. This required many blood tests, which eventually caused scar tissue to develop in the veins of both arms, making the tests a more difficult and painful process. A lot of time was also spent in allergy testing. Fortunately, the allergens used there were free of the glycerine I was allergic to. It took several hours each day as they stuck you with all kinds of allergens, one at a time, to see how you reacted. It was another huge room filled with suffering people waiting turns for each injection, then the reaction, then another injection, another reaction, and on and on. By the time the afternoon was over you could bank on being pretty sick. The next day you started the routines all over again.

Because I had nowhere else to turn, I tried all the treatments suggested, no matter what the cost. What did money matter if I was dead? They had all kinds of new age medicine and, in my ignorance, I tried them, too. An acquaintance suggested I make an appointment with the homeopathic doctor on the staff, so I did. I told her my medical history and how the allergy testing was making me sick. She said she had an easy way to check for allergies. She handed me a vial, that was 99.9% water, and told me to hold it tight, and she would try to pry my finger loose. If she could remove my finger from around the vial, then I was allergic to that substance. As I looked at her, I must have smirked. It all seemed so ridiculous. She stopped, looked up at me, and said, "Oh, you don't believe this?" I answered that it seemed a bit strange to me. I asked how the contents of the glass vial could possibly be affecting me. She went into this long and illogical explanation. Wanting to get out of there as soon as I could, I said no more and foolishly finished the testing. That night when I told Joe what I had done he was shocked that I had spent good money on this. He told me it was "bunk." I told him I was so desperate I was trying everything, but, of course, he was right! The "works of man" from which I sought healing now included superstition and outright fantasy. We did not know who the Healer was.

As time went on and I got worse, they suggested a new experimental and expensive treatment. Some of your blood is taken and changed in the lab to make your T-cells strong. The process took about two weeks. Then you would inject yourself with the transformed blood every few days. They told me there were risks involved, and that this treatment was very new. I was afraid of this, but, because I was so desperate, I decided to try it. The whole process made me very ill, but I plowed ahead. My vial of blood was sent to the lab and I waited for it to be ready—another hope to cling to.

Weekend Escape

On weekends the clinic was closed. My back was in better shape from my daily physical therapy, and I was able to drive. Even though I could not stay long in most places, I was usually able to go into movie theaters.

Joe and I would go to the movies often. It was about the only thing we could do. I was also able to go into a number of restaurants. That was also a treat. I got a map of this huge city. I was determined to find my way around and do things on the weekend in spite of how I felt. I poured over the map and the phone book and charted directions coming and going to most of the movie theaters in the city. Every weekend I went to a movie. No one went with me. They were too afraid, so I went by myself.

A Family Lunch

One day some of my family passed through town. I met them for lunch at a restaurant that I thought would be environmentally acceptable. It was good to see them, but I will never forget the painful, lonely, sinking feeling as I stood watching them drive from the parking lot after our good-byes. I remember thinking, "How long will I have to be here, and what is going to become of me?" I am sure others could feel the cape of hopelessness that surrounded me.

Joe Toils on Another House for Us

While I was in Texas Joe continued to work on our house. Joe and his friend, Virgil, removed the gas furnace and all the old duct work from inside the walls and installed a new system. It was a tremendous undertaking. Virgil had recently retired, and had worked with Joe for many years. He came to the house nearly every day for over a month to work on this project, with no pay or reward other than what God will surely give him. Terri and Joe's brother, Mike, Rita, and her husband, Carl, also helped. We felt an all-electric house would be better for my allergies. Rita's daughter, Michelle, and sons, Carl and Ross, came at one point and helped scrub all the woodwork and walls in the house, even the ones with old wallpaper on them. We did not think we could paint or redecorate. One bedroom was bright orange, and another was bright blue with huge white flowers covering the walls. Even though this was not my taste, I would have been grateful to live in our newly purchased ranch house—a place of our own.

51

CHAPTER 8

A FLICKER OF HOPE

M y food allergies became so severe that my weight dropped to ninety-nine pounds. I looked like "death walking." The clinic had me on an extreme rotation diet that required I not have the same food more than once in seven days. What to eat became a daily preoccupation, a search for something I had not eaten before which I might be able to tolerate. For one meal I had only radishes and lettuce. I was hungry all the time. I was eating rare, exotic foods just to stay alive. In one organic food store near the clinic, they sold frozen zebra, lion, and ostrich meat at very high prices. I had eaten a lot of organic food in the past, but now everything I ate had to be organic. At one point we had to acquire some of my food by mail order. Finding enough food to stay alive and that I was not allergic to was impossible. Each day was filled with incredible fear, stress, and anxiety. I lost all hope of getting well.

My weight was at an all-time low, and I was afraid I was dying. I saw people at the health center who were allergic to all types of food, and I knew that was happening to me. One woman at the clinic was down to one food. She could only eat turkey, so she ate it for all three meals. We all knew that eventually she would not be able to eat even that! When this happened the doctor sent people to the hospital where they would be fed through a central line surgically placed under their collarbone. The price was $1,000 a day, and insurance would not pay for this! I told a friend that I would not do this—enough was enough. I told her I would die first, and I meant it. I could not stand the thought of it and had heard a lot of horror stories about it. I just could not keep this up. I was completely hopeless and in the depths of despair. I felt death was just around the corner. A family member told me later that the family knew I was dying, but just never spoke of it. This is where dependence on myself and on human solutions had led me.

God Pursues

Right before I left for home I heard about a seminar on environmental illness that was being held that weekend in Houston, hosted by a non-denominational Christian healing ministry. It was about how God could heal this and many other diseases. I totally rejected it. Anyway, I was too ill to travel to Houston. It was three hours away, and I would have no way back to the clinic. I was just too sick to be healed! The flier about the conference had information about spiritual roots and blocks to healing among other things. It all sounded so strange to me. I knew chemical poisoning was my main problem. Kathy Herrmann, another patient at the clinic whom I had befriended, wanted to go and told me she knew this was the answer. I told her she ought to go if she felt that strongly about it. Even though I did not say it to her, I knew she would be wasting her time. What could a ministry know about health issues? She left for the conference while I secretly shook my head and thought she was really grasping at straws!

The hardest phone call I had to make was to Joe telling him to come get me. The clinic could not help me. In fact, they had made me worse. I told him there was no hope now. Truly all the solutions which man had to cure my illness had now been exhausted. It was very depressing. Joe said he would fly down to drive me back home. I could only imagine what he was thinking and feeling. I knew I was going home to die.

A Divine Appointment

I talked to a woman I barely knew one afternoon in the doctor's office while we both received our nutrient IVs. After she returned home she mailed me Merlin Carothers' book, *Power in Praise*, and a couple of worship music tapes which arrived the day before I left for home. I managed to read the first few chapters.[1] The book was about the power of praising God and how He heals when you turn to Him. It also told about many miracles. I had never read anything about this before, and even though I felt some faith stirring in me, I wondered if it was true. Did Jesus really heal today? Was He really that involved in our lives?

After spending three months at the clinic, separated from Joe, and after spending many thousands of dollars for treatment, some of it painful and risky, I was coming home in even worse condition. I knew there were people the clinic had helped, but many left worse than when they arrived because the treatments were so radical. There is no medical cure for environmental illness. I now acquired an oxygen tank for the trip home, which I had not needed before. I was filled with my all too familiar despair. I could hardly eat without having terrible reactions. My esophagus would close. My circulation would shut down. I got blinding head pains, which lasted for hours. I was worn out and did not know how I was going to go on. I had fought for years to get well, but I was definitely running out of energy for this struggle.

I did not know how I was going to make the trip home and stay in the car all those hours. I was so sick. I thought about trying the suggestions in the *Power in Praise* book and maybe that could get me home. I had read just enough to get the idea, and I had tried everything else. As I was lying in the back of the van, I was praying. All the way home, I was praising and thanking God for, and despite, my horrible situation. It seemed very strange to me, but that is what the book said to do—to thank God for all things (1 Thess. 5:16–18). I knew God did not do this *to* me, but He could certainly change things *for* me. So I was thanking and praising God, telling Him that I knew that He knew best, and that He would bring good from this. I did this under my breath hour after hour until I was home. Joe never knew what I was doing. I was amazed at how few reactions I had. I did not even need the oxygen. I could not believe I was able to get home without getting worse. *I realized I was on to something!*

Before we left the clinic they gave me my expensive blood solution and told us it had to be refrigerated or it would not be usable. Joe fixed the cooler, and I watched as he put the solution inside a plastic bag, zipped the bag shut, and placed it on ice in the bottom of the cooler. When we arrived home the blood vial was not there. Joe found it later under the back seat of the van, and not in the plastic bag. It was very strange. We *knew* it had been in the cooler, but somehow it did not arrive there. We could not figure out how it got out of the bag or the cooler. I thought about calling the clinic for more, but just never did. I was uncomfortable at the thought of this treatment anyway, so that made it easier for me not to call. I wondered if I was making a mistake, but decided to risk it. I hated the fact that more money had been wasted.

Before returning home I had spoken with my daughter about our living arrangements. She decided she would move out of the apartment and stay with a friend of hers. We felt it would be best for both of us. She could get back to a normal life and I could have complete quiet and privacy in a relaxed environment free from distractions. I really appreciated the fact that Terri made this sacrifice for me. I believe this solitude made it possible for me to do what I needed to do toward healing.

Back Home

When we got back home there was a message from Kathy. At the Houston seminar, she had seen people that were healed by God from environmental illness and wanted to tell me about it. I could not believe what I was hearing. She was telling me about people totally healed of this incurable disease and living normal lives. Miracles! I felt faith *bursting* inside of me. I had never known anyone who was miraculously healed. We were both filled with excitement as she told me everything she saw. After that, I started reading the Bible every day and thanked God daily that He was healing me. I praised and thanked Him continually. I also read as many inspirational books as I could find. I was on a new path for wellness!

CHAPTER 9

KEYS TO HEALING

Surrendered at Last

One afternoon in early October 1996, not long after returning from Texas, I sat down and had a talk with God. I finally realized I had been trying to do this myself, and without any success. I said, "Okay, God, I'm yours. I'm either going to die or I'm going to get well. I'm in your hands. I am through seeking doctors about it. I am through worrying about it, trying useless treatments, through struggling and fearing. I just can't do it anymore. I'm putting my life in your hands and turning everything over to you." I said the following prayer that was in a Merlin Carothers' book:[1]

> Dear God, I confess that I am a sinner. Please forgive all my sins—the ones I can remember and the ones I can't remember. Thank You, Jesus, that You lived a sinless life and took the punishment for my sins. I receive You as my Savior and the free gift of eternal life that You give me. I want to live for You, to serve You, and to honor You. I receive Your Holy Spirit and I will follow You.

I accepted Jesus into my life and heart in a new way. After that, I felt a burden lift from me. I actually felt some hope and joy. I began to realize that, although I had been a church-going Christian my whole life, my faith was weak. I did not really have a personal relationship with Jesus.

Over the next few weeks I wondered what I had done, turning my life over to God. I finally asked Him, "What does this mean to turn my life over?" He immediately answered me—so suddenly it amazed me. I had never heard a word from God before. He said, "On earth as it is in heaven." I thought of The Lord's Prayer. "Thy will be done, on earth as it is in heaven" (Matt. 6:10).

Holy Spirit Comes!

The Holy Spirit came into my life in a new, more powerful way. As I read the Bible, scriptures would leap off the page at me and I wrote them down on index cards. I loved the Word! I could not wait to read the Bible from cover to cover. I wanted to know all that was in it. I was amazed at God's promises. I was surprised at all the information and direction for living that was in the Bible. I was stunned at all the knowledge I had been missing because I was not studying God's Word. I saw that the Bible shows us how God wants us to live our lives. I realized in a deeper way that the Holy Spirit had actually written this book, through human authors, to guide us. As 2 Timothy 3:16 says, "All Scripture is given by inspiration of God." I saw God's view of right and wrong, which is quite different from the world's view. What a revelation!

From Scripture I began to realize the battle was in my mind, and that I needed to take every thought captive (2 Cor. 10:5). What I think influences what I say and how I feel because the mind and body are connected. We cannot dwell on negative things, mull over all the wrongs that have been done to us, cry in our pillow every night because all our needs are not met, and because our life is not what we thought it would be. We cannot do this and be healthy. From now on I was going to think and speak only what God said about healing in the Bible.

Conviction About Movies and Entertainment

I learned that accepting Jesus into my heart caused the Holy Spirit to move into my spirit in a very powerful way. As the Holy Spirit started working within me, I was being cleansed and sanctified by the Word of God, just as it is written in the Bible (Eph. 5:26). It was remarkable!

Soon after praying the prayer to give my life to Jesus, the Holy Spirit started dealing with me about many things in my life. One of the first was the movies I was seeing. I had always loved movies and everything connected with them. If it got a good critical review and appeared interesting to us, Joe and I went, regardless of the rating. After all, we were adults, this was just make-believe, and the movies were well done according to the world's view. The Bible says the eye is the light of the body (Matt. 6:22), and I was definitely seeing and taking things into my spirit that I should not have. I was seeing violence, which I always hated, and sin portrayed in an acceptable way.

Joe and I had been going to the movies almost once a week. It was one of the few things I was able to do. We would sit in the very back row and put our coats over the seats in front of us so that no one would sit near us. If someone wearing perfume sat near us I would need to leave. Joe always remarked that he did not know why some people wanted to smell like a pine tree!

When the Holy Spirit came into my life in this new way a change came over me. On the first weekend after my new, spirit-led conviction was established, Joe wanted to go to the movies. I told him I would not see that particular show. This was very difficult for me to do. He was a little agitated and puzzled over this. I remember him saying to me, "What am I supposed to do?" I said I did not know, but that I would not go to that movie and I hoped he could accept this. I tried to explain it to him and, even though he did not like it, he honored it. Each week I would carefully read the movie reviews hoping to find something acceptable that we could see. After a period of time, I knew the Lord did not want me seeing "R" rated movies no matter what movie star was in it or what wonderful things were said about it. Later, after Joe started reading the Bible himself, he was in full agreement with me and realized how corrupting many movies and TV programs are. From reading the Bible himself, he now knew this kind of entertainment was unacceptable in God's eyes.

We always went to the movies with Joe's brother, Jim, and his wife, Anthea, when they came to visit from Colorado. Joe and I discussed our lifestyle change with them. When we explained to them why we were being more selective, they could not have been nicer. We were grateful for their love and understanding.

Keys to Healing

Forgiveness—Important Key for Healing

In the first month of my quest for healing, the Holy Spirit told me I should apologize to someone whom I had unintentionally hurt in a major way. I did not want to do it and wondered if this was really God, as it might stir up a lot of things best forgotten. I fought this idea for almost three weeks using excuses like I could not go over to that person's house, or the house would make me sick, or they would not see me anyway. More time passed, and then the Holy Spirit gave me the idea of calling that person. I said, no, that I could not do that. It would be too hard. I knew I would start crying, or they might hang up on me. More time passed. The Holy Spirit then told me to write a letter of apology. I felt this was something I could do and immediately answered, "Yes, I can do that." I bought special stationery and envelopes, and after a few drafts, I finished the letter. It was not easy. I wrote the truth about how wrong I was in a certain situation, and I asked for forgiveness. This was difficult for me, but when I knew this was God's will, I was committed to being obedient. I walked to the mailbox and dropped it in. I was nervous, but relieved.

Two months later I received a reply and a note of forgiveness. I then knew the Lord wanted to free that person from unforgiveness toward me, and my apology facilitated that release. I would never have remembered or done this if the Holy Spirit had not intervened. I believe this was a block to healing that had to be removed.

It is true that the Holy Spirit never forces us to do anything against our will. At the same time, this was a very powerful encounter, and the Holy Spirit did not leave me alone during that time until I had an understanding of the importance of apologizing and forgiveness. I accepted the need to put down my pride and apologize.

Pleasant Valley Ministry—A Healing Ministry

Kathy Herrmann called again and insisted that I call the transdenominational Christian healing ministry south of Atlanta that she had

59

discovered. She was wise enough to attend that Houston seminar conducted by Pleasant Valley Ministry that I had quickly rejected. She said that Pastor Henry Wright had a great gift of knowledge of the spiritual roots of disease, and that thousands of people had been healed through his ministry. God was using this pastor in a major way. He was an expert on environmental illness and many other diseases. He had discovered the spiritual roots to many diseases and had found many spiritual blocks to healing. He taught that many people are not healed when prayed for because they have not dealt with the spiritual roots and removed the blocks.

Calling this ministry was not an easy thing for me. It was outside my religion. I thank God that He gave me the grace to call them. I probably would not be alive today if I had not taken this step.

On October 8, 1996, after my talk with Kathy, I called Pleasant Valley Ministry. They were wonderful! After that initial call, I had a phone appointment with them once a week. They would answer my questions, counsel, and pray for me. When I was growing up I was not encouraged to privately read the Scriptures. The ministry urged me to read the Bible every day and soak in God's Word. I was glad I had already started this on my own. I began in the New Testament, reading about how Jesus healed all the oppressed and sick who came to Him. The Holy Spirit was teaching me and feeding me things necessary for my survival and healing. The more I read and studied the more I wanted to learn. A whole new world opened up to me. I was like a dry sponge soaking up everything in my path. The Word of God was renewing my mind, and I was becoming spiritually alive! I spent many hours each day reading the Word of God, and it filled me with hope and faith to receive my healing. There is healing power in God's Word—like medicine—and I made sure I took my medicine morning, noon, and night (Prov. 4:20–22).[2] *The Bible, the Holy Word of God, was the most powerful instrument in my healing.*

I was advised to find a Bible-based, full gospel church that taught the Word and believed in healing. I had no desire to do this as I was content with my church, and I did not do anything about it immediately. Then I learned of a nearby church that would meet these requirements. Rita went with me one Saturday night to investigate. We did not care for it, and as we left we laughed and remarked that we had tried. We were very glad to scamper back to our own church. I never looked again for anything else. It just did not interest me.

The ministry also counseled me on the spiritual roots of my illness and on the spiritual blocks to healing. One of those roots was a broken heart. In my private reading of the Scriptures, before I had called Pleasant Valley Ministry, the Holy Spirit brought Proverbs 17:22 (NAB) to my attention: "A joyful heart is the health of the body, but a depressed spirit dries up the bones." I immediately knew this scripture was for me. I wrote it on a Post-it Note, and put it on my bathroom mirror. Later I learned that the Holy Spirit had shown Pastor Wright this same scripture six years earlier as the key to unlocking environmental illness! I also had Psalm 91:14–16 (NAB) posted on the mirror: "Whoever clings to me I will deliver, whoever knows my name I will set on high. All who call upon me I will answer; I will be with them in distress; I will deliver them and give them honor. With length of days I will satisfy them and show them my saving power." I read these scriptures and many others daily. They filled me with hope.

I listened to many hours of Pastor Wright's teaching tapes. I prayed for my healing everyday. I prayed healing scriptures and God's promises back to Him daily.[3] I prayed every day for faith to believe in healing. I prayed Mark 9:24 (NAB), "Lord I believe; help my unbelief."

I was told not to focus on my symptoms no matter how bad I felt. I was to believe and have faith that it was God's will to heal, and that He was healing me. God's Word is true, and I stood on that Word every minute of every day. As I sat before a plate of food, all of which I was allergic to, I prayed. I prayed Exodus 23:25 (NAB), "The Lord, your God, you shall worship; then I will bless your food and drink, and I will remove all sickness from your midst." I prayed scriptures before eating and did spiritual warfare while I ate as symptoms came upon me time and time again. As the months passed, the symptoms slowly lessened.

Allergies usually get worse if left untreated, but mine were improving! I believed that God was healing me. I continued praying and battling until the healing of my allergies was complete.

I thanked God daily for healing me even though, in the beginning, there was no strong evidence that He was. I made positive scriptural proclamations countless times everyday. Proverbs 18:21 says, "Death and life are in the power of the tongue." I stated things the way I wanted them to be, not the way they were (Rom. 4:17). I listened to and sang praise and worship music to God daily.

Repentance was also a key to healing. I went through my life and repented for anything I might have done to separate myself from God, no matter how small or seemingly insignificant, using the Scriptures as a guide.

I fed on the Scriptures. I spent many hours reading the Bible, and I made so many scriptural proclamations during the day that when I woke up in the middle of the night scriptures were running through my mind. I was soaking in the Word of God even in my sleep! Whenever I awoke in the middle of the night, I always prayed for faith. "Lord, give me faith for healing." I was asking and thanking, asking and thanking. I would be in so much pain as I stood over the stove cooking my food, yet I would praise and thank God for healing me. It seemed strange to me to thank Him for healing me when I was so sick, but I knew this was the right thing to do. I just believed that in time, His time, I would appropriate that healing He got for me on the Cross (Isaiah 53:4–5), and I would finally be well. I was going to do my part to help that happen.

Broken Heart Finally Healed

One day I realized that my severe broken heart over my son's death was gone. Yes, I missed him, but it was now a normal sorrow. The horrible brokenness I suffered with for years lifted. I had not been praying for that at all. God just reached into all the shattered places in my heart that had to do with Paul and healed them. I was so thankful when I realized this. Pastor Wright's ministry had told me that you have to heal

Keys to Healing

from the inside out. Your heart has to heal before your body can. God's love for me was becoming very real.

The Importance of "Soaking" Prayer

On October 24, 1996, sixteen days after calling Pleasant Valley Ministry, I discovered Francis MacNutt's book, *Healing,* in a Christian bookstore. I was immediately drawn to it. I could not read it fast enough.[4] That book, the Scriptures, and Pastor Wright's ministry are what really gave me the faith to seek a complete healing.

My family gathered one evening, and nine people prayed for me for an hour and a half. We got the idea from Francis MacNutt, who promoted *soaking*, extended prayer for healing.[5] That evening after I returned home I had some dramatic healing and improvement in my back, and we had not even prayed for that. Even though my back was not totally healed that night, what I did get was truly a miracle!

A few weeks later, on November 11, Francis MacNutt's Christian Healing Ministries in Jacksonville, Florida, put me on their intercessory prayer list. I read all of his books, as well as other books on the subject of healing. I read everything I could get my hands on to inspire me. I also continued to listen to many teaching tapes and prayed, prayed, prayed.

I could not wait to share with people the things I was learning about healing. I now knew of many miracles, people who had been healed from incurable medical problems. Many I cared about had serious health problems. I wanted to share the truths I had learned about healing, in the hope that they, too, would be healed. Many have since had healings of their own.

Freemasonry

A Block to Healing

I read many testimonies of healing that people sent me. A number of these people recommended Derek Prince's book, *Blessing or Curse, You Can Choose.*[6] They said it was a book with important information for their

63

healing. I read and followed his suggestions and said all of the prayers. One of the things I dealt with was a pillbox from the Eastern Star, the women's branch of Freemasonry, that had belonged to a relative. I had carried it in my purse for years. Several of my relatives and ancestors had belonged to the Masons. The Holy Spirit led me to destroy and dispose of the gold pillbox. I also repented for having it. I believe this was one of the blocks to my healing that needed to be removed.

Many people do not realize the implications of Freemasonry. I have read that those who have reached the higher levels have gone through many pagan teachings, rituals, and oaths. In the past, some Masons even drank from a human skull in many rites. Due to the secrecy, those in the lower levels do not realize what the organization really stands for, or its pagan roots. According to Ron Campbell, author of *Free From Freemasonry*, you will find none of the secret information on the Masonic Web sites and promotional brochures.[7] They only put out what they want the public to know. Campbell states, "Though millions of good men join the Lodge for honorable reasons, that doesn't make the Lodge good." He says "dozens of nineteenth-century Masonic scholars hold to the theory that the Masonic mysteries are deeply rooted in the mystery religions of Egypt, Greece, and Rome."

Jack Harris, a former Worshipful Master and author of *Freemasonry, The Invisible Cult in Our Midst,* states that everything is taught orally, nothing can be written down. Its mysteries are to be kept secret. Telling the Masonry "secrets" is considered a violation and brings painful, physical penalties. "These penalties are secret rituals and are given by word of mouth only." The organization does not want the world, especially the Christian community, to have a chance to evaluate the real and true character of this cult. Harris quotes John Quincy Adams, who was President of the United States from 1825–1829. Adams spoke out against Masonry in 1826 in letters and in his address to the people of Massachusetts:[8]

> I saw wine drank from a human skull with solemn invoca-
> tion of all the sins of its owner upon the head of him who
> drank it. I saw a wretched mortal man dooming himself to

eternal punishment when the last trump shall sound, as a guarantee for idle and ridiculous promises. Such are the laws of Masonry, such are their indelible character, and with that character perfectly corresponds the history of Masonic lodges, chapters, encampments and consistories, from that day to the present.

Coming from a Catholic background I was interested in the Catholic Church's view of the Masons. The revised 1917 Code of Canon Law issued in 1984 states that a sanction could be imposed on Catholics who join associations that work against the Church. The Sacred Congregation for the Doctrine of the Faith clarified the matter by publishing a declaration indicating that Catholics joining the Masons are involved in serious sin.[9]

Disposing of objects connected with these kinds of organizations can cause problems and draw criticism from those who lack understanding. They think you are being extreme. I would not keep any possession I thought might separate me from God. The Word of God gave me strength to know what was right. This was a block to healing, and I was willing to deal with it. No *thing* is worth separating myself from God and His loving grace and peace. I very much appreciated Pastor Wright praying with me in regard to this.

Rita's Faithfulness

My sister, Rita, visited me daily for many months, laying hands on me and praying for my healing. Our first prayer session was on Sunday, November 3, 1996. We had no previous experience, knowledge, or instructions in this type of prayer. Initially, I did not know of anyone who had been healed of a serious illness. Even though, in the past, we all prayed for God to intervene, we really did not know that Jesus actually heals today.

I was cautiously hopeful as Rita and I learned, with God's help and Francis MacNutt's books, how to pray for healing. The first time we prayed together like this we felt awkward and unnatural, but with each day it became easier and more natural. Because of my severe food allergies, I asked Rita to lay hands on my abdomen when we prayed. As Rita would place her hand on me, we would pray together from information in MacNutt's book. We prayed whatever we felt should be prayed in the name of Jesus.

We followed many of MacNutt's suggestions. We were being led by the Holy Spirit, but did not realize how much. Sometimes, as we prayed, I would feel a lot of heat in exactly the spot where Rita had her hand. We had read about this phenomenon, so we believed it was the healing presence of the Holy Spirit. That excited us. Rita was encouraging and very supportive, and I will be forever grateful for her faithfulness. She never lost hope that I would be well. When she first told me the prophecy she received, "Mary will be well," I believed and had hope. But, as the years went by and I only got worse, I lost all belief in the message. But God's time is not our time. Seven years after Rita was told I would be well, God started healing me. But I had at last positioned myself to receive healing!

Taking Some Ground Back

During this time, as I gradually got better, I was able to do more things and run errands again. I was taking back ground that had been stolen from me. I was still living in the apartment, but I would drive over to our house to pick up the mail. As I approached the house and entered the driveway, I always made positive proclamations and thanked God for this house. I told the Lord that I knew I would be in this house when the time was right. I trusted Him. As time went on, my faith grew regarding living there. I knew I would be living in this house someday. I just had to keep believing and be patient. The Word of God was still renewing my mind. My negative thinking was being replaced with hope and belief in the blessings God had for me and had always wanted me to enjoy. I refused to speak any longer in a negative way about my circumstances. I became aware of all the negative words, laced with fear, many people spoke about their lives. They do not know about Bible principles and the power of the tongue. They speak and expect the worst and that is usually what they get. I decided I would not live that way anymore. I believed God's promises in the Scriptures were true. Living in victory—that is what I wanted from now on and I expected to get it!

One day in early 1997, I told Joe that I felt we should hire someone to take off all the old wallpaper and have the whole interior of the house painted and redecorated. Joe was reluctant to do this. He thought it was risky and might keep me from eventually moving in. I was losing all fear of this. I really felt like we should do this. Joe finally agreed. We had it all done and also removed the old green carpeting to expose nice hardwood floors underneath. The house was beginning to look beautiful, and I knew that I would be in it soon, all in God's time.

CHAPTER 10

LEARNING SPIRITUAL WARFARE

I n the summer of 1997, I was fortunate enough to spend one month in Georgia at Pleasant Valley Church and Ministry. Rita and her daughter, Michelle, drove me as far as Atlanta and then flew home. I drove on by myself to Molena, an hour south of Atlanta. I was filled with anticipation and a little nervous at what I was going to encounter. The ministry is fairly isolated in the country with clean, fresh air, beautiful trees, winding two-lane roads and very little traffic. I finally arrived at a nice campground with trailers lining the back. People in all stages of healing lived there. The offices were on the left and right side of the park entrance. Pastor Wright and his family lived across a little lake behind the office building in a very nice double-wide mobile home. My friend, Kathy, was already there. She had asked me to share a trailer and expenses for the month. Pastor had a very long waiting list, and by sharing I was able to go sooner.

The accommodations were tight. Usually only one person lived in each trailer. It was necessary for us to make some compromises since we were sharing. We decided to take turns with the queen bed that was up a few steps and the narrow sofa bed in the main section of the trailer. The bathroom was very tiny and maneuvering was difficult. The shower was also exceptionally small and, because of my height, it was difficult for me to enter and exit. Because there was a water shortage, we decided that I would take my shower every evening and Kathy would use the bathroom every morning. We both later agreed that sharing the small, close quarters was not ideal, especially since our stay was a month long. In spite of the inconveniences, we managed and were grateful for this opportunity that so many were waiting for. They have since built nice cabins where people can stay.

I got wonderful ministry from Pastor Wright and his staff. I was blessed to sit in on his daily Bible class. He taught the Word every morning for more than an hour. I felt privileged to be there and to learn from his teachings. He exhibited much wisdom and knowledge. I met several people whom God had healed, and many who were in the process of being healed from all kinds of illnesses.

Sin and Deception Revealed

I had not been there long before the Holy Spirit started dealing with me about the medal and the scapular that I had brought with me. Medals and scapulars are devotional objects, usually worn around the neck, with the image of a particular saint. Saints are people who had exhibited exemplary holiness during their lives and were believed to be in Heaven. These objects are used to assist one's praying to that saint to intercede with God to accomplish the purpose of the prayer. The Catholic Church has always promoted praying to the saints to intercede with the Lord on our behalf.

I was in turmoil most of one night over having these objects as I read the Scriptures, especially Deuteronomy 5:7–10, the first commandment, which forbids making images and giving them a place that only God should have. I also became concerned about praying to anyone but God. This seemed to conflict with several scriptural passages. For example, in 1 Timothy 2:5 it is written, "For there is one God, and one mediator between God and men, the man Christ Jesus." This Scripture clearly states that only Jesus intercedes for us to the Father.

Someone close to the family had given the scapular to me and I was told to wear it for protection. According to written information included with scapulars, wearing them in faith also assured salvation. That night I was led to the belief that this was superstition. Why did I not see this before now? The Catholic Church does not condone superstition, but this clearly was. I struggled with this all night. A lot of damage can be done by these practices, even to well-meaning and otherwise good Christians. It became clear to me that by using the medal and the scapular, I was acting contrary to the first commandment.

As I pondered this throughout the night, I began to feel sick and uncomfortable. I really felt tormented. I sealed the two images in an envelope and decided that I would repent and throw the envelope in the dumpster outside the office in the morning. I became very ill as I came under demonic attack for this decision. By morning, with the help of the Holy Spirit, I had no doubt that I was doing the right thing. As I left for Bible class I made sure I had the envelope. I did not tell anyone about it at that time.

That morning Pastor taught for one hour. Then, suddenly, he started teaching a spontaneous Bible lesson about idols and graven images. This was not a coincidence. He was definitely inspired by the Holy Spirit, and I knew this teaching was specifically for me. As he began to teach about graven images, I became very sick again. He taught another thirty minutes. It seemed like forever. When Pastor finished, I was so ill that I actually staggered up to the podium and said, "I'm in trouble." I told him I was sick, and that I had been tormented all night over a decision to throw away my medal and scapular. I held up the envelope and told him they were in it. I said again that I was extremely ill. I mentioned all of my symptoms. He told me that I was not sick, not in the normal sense. He told me where to sit, and he quickly dismissed the class, except for a few chosen people he asked to stay and pray. Pastor told the group, "She's really been tormented." He told them an evil spirit was manifesting, and that we would have a deliverance. Many thoughts were rushing through my mind. I could not believe this was happening to me—a Christian. I have since learned how common this is, and that many people, including Christians, need to be set free of many different things. They just do not know it. According to Archbishop Henry D'Souza of Calcutta, even the beloved and holy Mother Teresa was set free from an evil spirit causing insomnia.[1] As I sat where I was told, Pastor gave instructions. I felt horrible and began to cry softly. I felt like I was in some weird nightmare.

Learning Spiritual Warfare

I was confused and in shock. Pastor Wright sat in front of me on a desk stool. He looked squarely into my eyes and asked me to repeat something *in the name of Jesus*. I could not speak! No matter how hard I tried, I could not do it. He asked me some questions and then immediately started praying and quoting Scriptures. He asked me again to say, *in the name of Jesus*. I tried to form the words, but they would not come out of my mouth. I was shocked. My tongue was tied by something. He swung around and said to the others who were praying. "See, it is a spirit. When you are sick, you can still speak. This is an evil spirit."

He commanded the spirit to loose my tongue in the name of Jesus. I still could not speak. I was foggy-headed. I could not think clearly, and I had a hard time focusing and hearing what he was saying. I was having trouble comprehending. He announced again to the group that sickness does not prevent one from speaking. He rolled his chair closer, looked into my eyes, and told me what to say *in the name of Jesus*. I tried to form the words. Pastor kept quoting Scripture. I was finally able to speak the words with some difficulty and in slow motion. He read me scriptures and asked me to repeat them. I told him I was blocked. I told him I could not understand what he was saying even though these scriptures were familiar to me. Pastor said, "Of course you are—the spirit is blocking you—it is battling to win and remain." He continued to read scriptures. As the scriptures were quoted, my condition got even worse. He said that was because the Word of God has power and was stirring up the evil spirit. He was commanding the spirit to leave in the name of Jesus and called it by name. After praying and quoting scriptures for a few more minutes, there was no further manifestation.

I saw the *power* of the Word of God during this session. The Word of God was the weapon, the sword, against evil (Eph. 6:17). What a revelation that was! Evil spirits cannot stand against God's Word and a believer's authority backed by the power of the Holy Spirit (Mark 16:17). They have to go in the name of Jesus—another revelation. Of course, repentance was also a very important part of this. I had to repent to God for believing in and wearing these things which had opened the door for a demon to come into my life. Finally, Pastor felt the session was at an end. When it was all over, I was told not to be afraid. God was more powerful than any evil spirit. I left the office, repented again, and threw the envelope into the dumpster.

As I walked back to my trailer, I was in awe over what I had learned. God's Word is our weapon. Hebrews 4:12 says it is alive and powerful! Jesus Himself demonstrated the power of God's Word when Satan tempted Him in the desert after He fasted forty days. Jesus had victory over Satan by quoting Scriptures. He answered Satan's temptations with "It is written . . ." and spoke the Word of God (Matt. 4:1–11; Luke 4:1–13).

I gained tremendous knowledge on this trip to the ministry. I came away from this experience knowing more of the power in the Word of God. Ignorantly falling into superstitious ways and unknowingly breaking the first commandment opened the door for an evil spirit to come into my life. Not knowing it was wrong did not protect me. I suffered the consequences of my sin. I could not help thinking about all the people in the same situation.

Thank God the Holy Spirit is more powerful than any demon from hell. "For greater is He [Holy Spirit] that is in you, than he [the devil] that is in the world" (1 John 4:4). The Bible became even more precious to me.

Atlanta

My time at Pleasant Valley was over, and I said my goodbyes. I was so grateful for the wonderful help from these good, loving people. I met Joe in Atlanta, and we took a short vacation in the area before driving home. We had not been on a vacation in years. I was able to stay in several motels and visit many attractions in Georgia and Tennessee, including theaters, historical sites, and even a smoky country music show. I was walking out of my sickness to the other side—health and happiness.

Finally Home

Upon returning home in July 1997, from Pleasant Valley Ministry, I was able to move into the house that we had purchased three years earlier. Thank God—I was finally home.

Chapter 11

Healed!

I t took over a year to completely heal from my illness, but my allergies are now gone—completely healed by God. The Lord has given me my life back. I now go wherever I want, do what I want, and eat what I want without reactions. Even though I prefer organic food because it is healthier, when I shop at the supermarket or eat at a restaurant I do not worry if the food is pesticide free or not. I will never give in to that fear again.

I have gained my weight back and more. When I was sick I used to pass a mirror and pray that God would put some meat back on my bones. Now I pass a mirror and say, "Lord, enough already."

I wear whatever kind of clothes I want. They do not have to be only cotton like I used to require. I do not have to wash them ten times to get all the chemicals out before I can wear them. We bought some new furniture and have also reupholstered some old furniture with fabric chosen because we liked it, not because it was "safe" or free of chemicals. Freedom!

We remodeled our bathroom and used no special products, which are always twice the cost. We put in new wood cabinets, new tile using standard glue and grout, new drywall, fresh paint, and we did all this while I was living in the house! I have flown on airplanes, driven across the country, and stayed in motels. In September of 1999 my husband and I went to Italy for seventeen days for our wedding anniversary. This was something I never thought I would be able to do. I can go anywhere now regardless of the environment. My old fears and problems are gone. I never even think of them anymore. Thank God, that is all history!

I have learned many things through all this, but one thing is sure— if you seek healing you cannot be timid. Go boldly before the Throne

Healed!

(Hebrews 4:16) over and over again with persistent prayer. Never give up no matter how long it takes or how hopeless it looks. Ask and it will be given to you (Matt. 7:7).

I thank God that He continued to pursue me until I turned to Him. He never gave up on me. He is a God of love and second chances. I am thankful that He sent different people into my life to help me and enlighten me. He pursued me, wooed me, taught me, and healed me. What a loving God He is!

No doctor or alternative medicine or other works of man could accomplish my healing. But, God can do anything. God is our Healer, our Physician, our Deliverer.

Just when you think there is no one to help you, there He is, *lifting you up!*

> I will extol thee, O LORD; for thou hast lifted me up, and hast not made my foes to rejoice over me.
>
> O LORD my God, I cried unto thee, and thou hast healed me.
>
> O LORD, thou hast brought up my soul from the grave; thou hast kept me alive, that I should not go down to the pit.
>
> I cried to thee, O LORD; and unto the LORD I made supplication.
>
> Thou hast turned for me my mourning into dancing: thou hast put off my sackcloth, and girded me with gladness;
>
> To the end that my glory may sing praise to thee, and not be silent. O LORD my God, I will give thanks unto thee for ever.
>
> —PSALM 30:1–3, 8, 11–12

PART II

THE JOURNEY CONTINUES: MORE DISCOVERIES ABOUT HEALING

CHAPTER 12

FOLLOWING THE HOLY SPIRIT'S LEAD

Discovering Mike Bickle's Ministry

On November 1, 1997, I was led to a wonderful charismatic church, Metro Christian Fellowship (MCF) of Kansas City. God used Mike Bickle's book, *Passion for Jesus*, to accomplish this. A friend mailed me a copy after we had been mailing books and tapes back and forth for months. I was always taught that Jesus loved us, but Mike made it real and personal and gave me a more complete understanding. It has changed my life, and I will be forever grateful. After reading his book, I wanted to hear him preach. I was excited to learn that he was the Pastor of a church only fifteen minutes from where I lived. I asked Rita if she would go with me, as I did not want to go alone. I did not know what to expect. She agreed to go, and Joe also came with us. We walked into this large auditorium for the Saturday evening service. It was very different from my beautiful church with stained glass windows and comfortable, padded pews. This place had a large platform for the speaker and for the singers and musicians. There was a sea of hard, orange chairs and no windows at all. We quietly slipped into the back row. The worship music was also very different from the reverent old hymns to which I was accustomed. I loved the worship music and how we were talking directly to God, worshiping and praising Him. His presence was there. It was very exciting. I could see real love for the Lord on peoples' faces as they adored Him with all their hearts. I loved that!

Pastor Mike Bickle gave the sermon. We were a little puzzled by it.

He was talking about the "fragrance of God" and taught from the Song of Solomon. When we left we looked at each other, shrugged, and wondered what he was talking about, the fragrance of God? It was definitely over our heads. Even though I did not understand a lot of what he said, I knew I liked it!

The next Sunday Joe and I got up as usual and began getting ready to go to Mass. We had been attending Mass on Sunday all of our lives. As I finished dressing I had this strong stirring in me, a very definite pull to go back to the interdenominational church we had attended. I told Joe I was sorry, but I knew I had to go back to MCF. I really felt the leading of the Holy Spirit in this. Joe was wonderful. He told me to do whatever I felt I was supposed to do. He was not going to interfere with anything God was doing in my life. Joe had always been open-minded and knew that all believers in Jesus, regardless of denomination, made up the whole body of Christ. I was greatly blessed by his love and support. He never judged me or tried to change my mind. He trusted me to know when I was hearing from God.

As I entered the church and the worship started I felt this excitement rising in me. I had never before been excited about church. This place was so alive. After the service Pastor Bickle called the Prayer Ministry Team and anyone could come up for hands-on prayer for healing or any need. This was such a wonderful opportunity for people. I felt blessed being there.

"Led" Again

The next Sunday the same thing happened. I knew I was supposed to go back. Joe again was very considerate. This was the first time in all our married life that we were not going to church together. He went to Mass and I went to what I called the "Healing Church."

While I immediately loved this new church, I was in a little turmoil over leaving my comfort zone, my life-long religion, and going someplace completely different for the first time in my life. It was difficult taking those first steps, mainly because I was not going to church with Joe. Even though I felt right at home from the very beginning, it was an adjustment. As I drove down the freeway to church by myself, I wondered what I was doing. How strange this seemed, striking out like this. I had not been interested in finding a new church, and I would never have done this on my own. I had promised God that I would do His will, and I knew this was His will for me. It was such a strong leading of the Holy Spirit that, in spite of some conflicting thoughts, it made it easy to be obedient, and I never looked back. I had no desire to return to my former church. I knew God had to be in this, and, as time went on, it became very evident that He was.

It turned out to be one of the best things I have ever done. There was now tremendous joy in my heart surrounding going to church, something I had never experienced before. The Lord does know best! I made many good friends there, people I respect. This church, which has a healing ministry, is where some of my family and I have experienced additional healings. The Lord is continually blessing me! There are many Biblical principles I would not know today if I had not heard the teachings there. Mike Bickle's passion, revelations, and teaching have inspired me and spoiled me. About a month after I started going to MCF, Rita started attending with me. She grew to love it as much as I did.

Terri's Dramatic Healing of Asthma

In the beginning, my daughter, Terri, was a little disturbed that I was going to this new church. I tried to explain to her about the leading of the Holy Spirit. She accepted it even though it was new to her and something she did not completely understand. Terri was going through a very hard time. She had struggled with pneumonia that had triggered a very serious and stubborn bout of asthma. It went on for months, and she even had to give up her job. There were many trips to the doctor and much medication. She had never had asthma before even though she had suffered with bronchitis numerous times. Asthma and bronchitis run in the family.

Terri was so seriously ill that her doctor thought, more than once, that he would have to hospitalize her. I approached Terri about coming for healing prayer at the church. I explained the hands-on prayer, and that this was a very safe place. She was hesitant, since this was not her church. I convinced her that she had nothing to lose and that I would go with her. I told her these were devout Christians who knew the Word of God and believed that Jesus heals today. She agreed because she trusted me and because of her desperate situation.

That night it was bitter cold and icy, but I was determined to go in spite of the weather conditions. We did not see many cars on the road as we crept along at a slow speed. The prayer meeting was held at the church office building. Because of the weather, there was no one else waiting for prayer. Pastor Lee Harms, a caring, gifted man, and his talented wife, Doris, led the prayer group.

When Terri explained to him about her asthma and the seriousness of it, he said, "We have had very good success with God healing asthma. We have discovered that it can be a spirit of infirmity that has attached itself to the lungs." He was very gentle and careful telling us this. He did not want to frighten us, and he also did not know how much we knew about this aspect of healing. Many churches today do not teach about evil spirits, even though Jesus and the apostles encountered them regularly in their healing ministries. In fact, just before Jesus ascended into heaven, He stated that one of the signs of a believer was that they would drive out demons in His Name (Mark 16:16–18). I knew about all of this and had prepared Terri for this possibility.

Pastor Lee gathered the intercessors around, and they started praying for Terri. He then rebuked the spirit of infirmity and commanded it to leave in the name of Jesus. He cast it out. This took a very short time. Terri felt it leave and lift from her. Lee discerned that it was gone and started to say, "It's gone," when, at just the same moment, Terri also said, "It's gone." Terri was dramatically delivered and healed of asthma that evening on December 9, 1997.

Within the next few days, Terri went to her doctor. He was amazed at the condition of her lungs. He could not believe how clear they were. He immediately cut her medicine in half. Terri knew she was healed but went along with her doctor. He had her come back again later and then took her off all medication. He had previously told Terri that she might be on one of the medications (an inhaler) for years. Through deliverance, God had healed her lungs of asthma. Her doctor still comments, with amazement, on her healing.

Later I asked Terri what she thought of this church now? She was all smiles. She had been set free, and whom the Lord sets free is free indeed (John 8:36)! Not long after that, Terri and her husband, Mike, decided to join Metro Christian Fellowship themselves. I believe they both found something there they needed.

My First Christian Conference

In January 1998, Rita and I signed up for our first conference at the church. It was titled Healing, Exploring Principles, Experiencing Power, with Dr. Jack Deere, Paul Cain, and Dr. Sam Storms. The teaching was excellent, and it covered a subject I was very interested in.

Word of Knowledge

On the last day of the seminar, there was a gentleman who came up to the front with a word of knowledge (1 Cor. 12:8). It was a word about a very specific matter that I had been praying for. I did not stand up at first. I wondered if this could really be for me? Not one person out of the two thousand people stood up, so he announced it a second time. As I got up, I looked around. I was the only one in an audience of two thousand people who stood. I was amazed that God was speaking specifically about me and only me! A man, Greg, approached me saying he felt that he should pray for me. I discovered that God had also healed him of environmental illness (EI). There were many intercessors present, but he was the only one who walked up to me. Another woman walked up and listened to us talking. It turned out that she was desperately ill and struggling with EI. It was very unusual that the three of us connected with EI were somehow all standing together in that large crowd. When he finished praying for me, we prayed for this woman. I was able to share my testimony of healing with her and later send her some information on healing of EI. I was impressed at how God has a way of bringing people together. He watches over us all.

Instant Healing Through Cindy Jacobs

In April of the same year my sister, Rita, and I attended the Women and the Prophetic III seminar at the church. Rita had been suffering for one year with a very painful bone spur on the heel of her foot. She could not walk barefoot across a hard surfaced floor or wear certain shoes without pain. Three days before Rita was to drive me to Pleasant Valley Ministry in Georgia this condition came upon her. During the first evening of the conference, Cindy Jacobs, a guest speaker from Colorado, had a word of knowledge about bone spurs. She said God wanted to heal bone spurs that night. Cindy had us all stand and said a general prayer over the whole congregation for this. Neither Rita nor I thought much about it. It was at least a month or more after the seminar before Rita finally told me that her bone spur had been completely healed that night. She waited to say anything because she wanted to be sure. All of her problems in her heel were gone after one prayer. She was completely and instantly healed by God.

Rita and I went to all the conferences at the church. We were hungry for the powerful presence of God demonstrated there, and for the education we received. The teachings were always good, and we were learning so much. We were continually blessed at these conferences, and we were in awe of the healings.

Eye Miraculously Healed

In November 1998, I attended the Shiloh conference at MCF on Releasing the Prophetic in the Local Church. There I experienced yet another healing! At that time, it had been over twelve years since I was accidentally hit in my left eye. The muscle in my eye was damaged, which caused the eyeball to occasionally "float." When I was tired I was unable to focus enough to read. It had become a real nuisance and was getting worse. During the past summer I had to make three separate trips to the eye doctor because the muscle problem had made it difficult to prescribe glasses correctly. Surgery was the only solution, but this was a last resort. Joe and I had been praying together for the healing of my eye for over a year. At one of the conference sessions there was a word of knowledge about God wanting to heal people who had double vision. People with this eye condition were asked to come to the front of the church for prayer. I did not go because it did not sound like my problem, but almost immediately I wished I had. At the last minute I finally asked for prayer. A husband and wife team prayed a very short prayer for my eye. I was happy to receive the prayer and a little hopeful. Even though there was no immediate evidence that any healing had taken place, I had some joy about it. As the days passed I realized that the eye had been healed—instantly! The symptoms, floating eye and inability to focus, had disappeared.

About a year later I went back to the doctor. I had not had any of my usual eye muscle problems in the past year and asked that he check the eye. He became excited as I passed each test. My eye muscle was now stable. I then told him how the symptoms had disappeared after prayer. He told my husband to take me out and celebrate. I knew he did not know quite what to think, but he was all smiles. Reversal of that problem was not possible without surgery.

Praying for Others

Rita and I decided we wanted to pray for others. The Lord had blessed us so much that it just seemed right to give back. On November 21, 1999, Rita and I were installed on the Metro Christian Fellowship Prayer Ministry Team after completing the required training. We could now pray for others at the church. We were also on a prayer team one evening a week for a few years, led by Associate Pastors Lee and Doris Harms of MCF, where we saw many healings, deliverances, and miracles take place. Today, Lee and Doris oversee the Heartland Healing Rooms at Christ Triumphant Church in Lee's Summit, Missouri, where they are now members.

Knees Instantly Healed

On January 28, 1999, during Thursday evening healing prayer at MCF, I experienced another healing! I did not go for prayer for myself, but intended only to pray for others. But, God wanted to include me in healing as well.

After completing prayers for everyone else who had come, I asked for prayer for my back and neck. A gentleman in the group had discernment regarding a different problem. He asked me if I had any joint pain. After I said yes, he asked if it was in my knees. Joe and I had been praying for the healing of my knees for a number of months. The problem in both knees came on quite suddenly. I had not been able to kneel down without severe pain. Getting up had been extremely difficult because of the weakness, stiffness, and sharp pains. This discerning gentleman and the prayer team laid hands on my knees and prayed for healing. Although I did not realize it at the time, I had a very dramatic and immediate healing. I did not notice any difference during or after prayer, as I only had pain when I knelt down. I did not think to try to kneel to test it. Two days later I was at church and everyone was asked to come up front and kneel for prayer. Immediately the thought ran through my mind that I could not do that because of my knees. Then I thought, "No, I *can* do that. I am healed." I walked up, knelt down, and hoped I could get back up. I got up easily with absolutely no struggling or pain in my knees. I was totally overwhelmed with God's goodness and mercy toward me, and I felt very blessed. I joyfully got on my knees and thanked the Lord for blessing me with yet another healing.

When I have a problem now, the first person I turn to is God Almighty. I know how much He cares about me. There is no doubt in my heart or mind that He is a healing God!

CHAPTER 13

THE GLORY REALM
IN CHICAGO

June 29–30, 2000—Benny Hinn Miracle
Crusade in Chicago at the United Center

J oe and I have taped Pastor Benny Hinn's television show, *This Is Your Day*, for a long time. Then we watch it when we have some free time. Watching the miracle crusades and all the healings are very inspirational. I noticed that Pastor Hinn was going to be in Chicago in June. This was the closest to Kansas City that I had seen him scheduled. Pastor Hinn mentioned that he knew by the Holy Spirit that the Chicago Crusade was going to be special. Joe casually mentioned that maybe we ought to go to one of his crusades sometime. I had wanted to go for a long time, so I immediately started checking on hotels and airfare. I talked to Rita and she wanted to go too. Terri was also interested. I approached Joe with all the information and we agreed we would go. I then made all the reservations for the four of us. As the time approached, Joe was becoming less enthusiastic about making this trip. He felt like it would be too much trouble and a lot of work. After talking to the Benny Hinn Ministry, I realized it would definitely be a hard trip. I was told people lined up hours in advance to make sure they could get in and get a good seat. At some of his crusades people are turned away due to lack of space. We knew the United Center in Chicago could hold more than twenty thousand people, so we were braced for this. Every now and then Joe mentioned he might not make the trip. My heart was set on doing this, so I held fast. I knew this was a rare opportunity, and I did not want to miss it. I had admired

86

The Glory Realm in Chicago

and been inspired by Benny Hinn ever since I read his book, *Good Morning, Holy Spirit,* in 1996 soon after I started seriously seeking God for healing.[1]

The experience of the crusade was indeed difficult. We stood in a long line outside in the hot sun waiting to get in. Each day we were able to get fairly good seats. The worship was wonderful, and Pastor Hinn's teachings were very good. Everything he taught was inspired, and built our faith for healing. We saw many miracle healings. Many came out of wheel chairs, which were lined up on the stage to inspire faith. We saw a number of people healed from emphysema, a lot of people healed of arthritis, and many other serious conditions. On the second day we sat next to a young girl who was healed from cystic fibrosis. There is nothing too difficult to heal for the God who created the universe!

Pastor Hinn told us on the first night not to miss any of the three sessions. On the last night of the Crusade, the Holy Spirit was moving powerfully through the auditorium. Pastor Hinn walked to the left side of the stage and told everyone to hold hands. He waved his hands toward them and told them to receive the Holy Spirit. The whole section of people fell down in a wave under the power of the Holy Spirit. It was quite a sight. He then walked to the other side of the stage and did the same thing. I had seen many people "rest" in the Spirit, but I had never seen anything like this. It was something to witness. Pastor Hinn always gave God the credit and the glory.

The Fragrance of God

Toward the end of the evening Pastor Hinn asked everyone to remain silent. He knew from the Holy Spirit that something unusual was about to happen. He then said we were going to smell the "fragrance of God." I knew of people who had smelled this when they were deep in prayer and private scripture study, but I never had. Then he said; "There it is, the fragrance of God. Do you smell it?" People in the front by the stage were waving and nodding that they could. I did not smell anything. Then, suddenly, there it was. It was like a sweet, heavy incense. Some said it smelled like frankincense. I took two deep breaths of the heavenly

87

fragrance, and then it was gone. All four of us smelled it. The fragrance seemed to move around the auditorium, and then it was over. This was a very special touch from the Lord.

Joe's Back Healed Through the Miracle Crusade

Joe had a nagging, painful back problem for years that flared up now and then. At times he could not stand long at all. It had become a real nuisance, and we had been praying for his healing for a long time. We found out that many people are healed waiting in line to get into the Benny Hinn Miracle Crusades, and some are healed on their way *to* the Crusade. That is what happened to Joe. The minute he got in the car to drive to the Crusade, God instantly healed his back! He now does things he had not been able to do for years, including lifting heavy objects, without pain. This was an undeniable miracle. We were in awe of the goodness and mercy of God—again.

CHAPTER 14

DIVINE HELP AT MY MOTHER'S DEATH

December 2000

My mother, age eighty-five, suffered with a heart condition and other health problems. She had been living in a retirement home for seven years. She lived the last two of those years on an assisted-living floor, as she needed help with medication and a number of other things. She always loved music and dancing, so she enjoyed the weekly parties very much. She also looked forward to eating and socializing with her friends in the dining room.

Mother's memory had declined during her last two years. She also had some confusion. But, there were many clear moments, and she could still hold a good conversation. I lived only five minutes from her, which was a real blessing, and toward the end I spent many hours with her. I took her to her doctor's appointments, got her supplies, shopped for her clothes, hunted for lost items, and took care of a lot of her emotional needs. My brother and each of my sisters also took a day a week to check on her and occasionally take her out to lunch, which she enjoyed. Mother was blessed with loving, caring children.

While she was still able to drive, she went to daily Mass and always prayed for everyone's needs. She was a woman of faith like her mother. The last year of her life she confided to me that she had a terrific fear of dying. She was really suffering over it. She agonized over burning in "purgatory" for many years before she would be cleansed and holy enough to enter Heaven. This belief was causing her a lot of stress, as she was eighty-four at the time and knew she was close to her eternity.

89

Purgatory, according to Roman Catholic doctrine, is a place or state of punishment wherein the souls of those who die in God's grace, but have minor or "venial" sins, may make satisfaction for these sins and become fit for heaven. It is an intermediate state after death for purification before entering heaven.[1,2]

Freedom From Fear

It was my pleasure to explain to her that she would not have to go through that because there was no such place as purgatory. I told her about a Catholic priest who had a weekly Bible class that I used to attend, who spoke about this in one of the sessions. He said purgatory was not mentioned in Holy Scripture, that the idea of purgatory was antiquated thinking, that it was unscriptural, and that there was no such place. He also said many Catholic theologians had abandoned the concept. I told her it pleased me when I heard this, as I had come to this conclusion on my own during my own study of the Scriptures.

I explained that Jesus died on the cross for our sins, and when we repent, confess our sins, and are sorry, that the sin is forgiven forever. The Bible says our sins will be remembered no more (Heb. 10:17). She believed that Jesus had died on the cross for her sins, but she did not understand the full truth because of this teaching about purgatory. I told her that there is nothing we, of ourselves, can do to atone for sins. Doing penance for forgiveness of sins was meaningless. Only Jesus' sacrifice can atone for sin. Jesus died for our sins once and for all (Heb. 7:27; 10:11–14). When we truly repent of sin, it is as if we had never sinned. Our sin is removed from us as far as the east is from the west (Psalm 103:12).

Mother was thrilled and asked a lot of questions, and we talked about it many times. It brought her such peace, and the horrible fear of dying, with which she was plagued most of her life, was gone. Mother was so grateful. We talked about many spiritual things during those last couple of years. She told me she believed that God had healed me of environmental illness, and she was in awe of that. She was now able to receive what God wanted her to have: peace, trust in Him, and the truth.

Divine Help at My Mother's Death

Mother had two angioplasty procedures on her heart that prolonged her life. She lived an extra two years after the second procedure. That is the time that she pursued more spiritual matters with me and came to peace over how much Jesus loved her. I convinced her that eternity was going to be more wonderful than she could even imagine or think.

The last two months of her life were extremely miserable, and she was ready to be with the Lord. Rita and I prayed even more with her during that time, and we visited almost daily.

I had been praying and asking the Lord for at least a year to let me be with Mother when she died. I knew her health was deteriorating, and so did everyone else. I did not want her to be alone, and I felt I could help her through it. She wanted me there, and it meant a lot to me to be there for her.

Prayers Answered

Joe and I had been praying for over a year that Mother would not have to move. We prayed that she would live in her apartment until the end of her days, and we trusted God to make that happen. I had put Mother in God's hands a long time ago and knew He was watching over her.

Mother had fallen many times the last two years of her life, but had never broken a bone in spite of having osteoporosis. The nurses could not understand that. They would mention it often. Joe and I knew! Falling was one of the things we prayed to God about. I finally told one of the nurses it was the power of prayer. She readily agreed that it would have to be so, because this was not normal. We knew she was protected through prayer in this regard. It really brought me peace.

Coping After a Stroke

In early December 2000, I was rushing over to sit with my mother while she ate her dinner. I did not want her eating all alone. She was suffering from not being able to go to the dining room anymore. As I stepped into the apartment, I noticed that it was unusually dark and quiet. I called her name. She answered from the bedroom and was very upset. I found her on the floor between the foot of her bed and the desk with her head under the corner of the bed. I pulled the emergency cord and then ran to the nurses' station to get help. Many times they were not in the office, so I was not going to lose any time. Thankfully, they were there this time. They ran back with me, and, with difficulty, helped her on to the bed. She had been unable to get up by herself, and we could not tell how long she had been lying there. It seemed like forever to her, and she was frightened. Her blood pressure was extremely high. I felt that she probably had a stroke. I called the family, and then I followed the ambulance to St. Luke's Hospital, wondering how I should pray. I knew she wanted out of this world, so I just prayed that God's will would be done, and that she would not suffer.

She indeed had a stroke. By the next morning she could not use the right side of her body and her speech was deteriorating. It was difficult to understand her. We never left mother alone. We all took turns staying with her day and night. After almost a week in the hospital, it became clear that they could not help her there. The doctors recommended we transfer mother to a skilled nursing facility for rehabilitation.

The next hurdle was where to put mother for rehabilitation. I really wanted her as close to home as possible, because I knew I would be spending many hours there. During the days she was in the hospital I prayed constantly for this. A wonderful social worker helped me select a place that mother's insurance would cover. One facility was only three minutes from my house and was highly recommended. We agreed that this was where we wanted her. The only hitch was that mother had to pass an evaluation from the director of nursing at the skilled nursing center. For the insurance company to pay for this they had to be assured that she could be rehabilitated. At this time mother was sleeping a lot because of the pain medication. She also was not very cooperative, and working at rehabilitation overwhelmed her. The evaluation time was set up for two days later.

I have never prayed so much in my life. I was in constant intercessory prayer while driving to and from the hospital, during all my time in the hospital, as well as at home. Almost everyone was doubtful that she could pass the test because of her condition. They could not even keep her awake long enough to eat. Yet, if the medication was withdrawn, she suffered too much. The doctor even changed the medication in the hope that she could stay awake longer, but the situation did not improve. The doctors and nurses were very puzzled by this since they had her on the lowest possible dose. The excessive sleeping was not normal, as they mentioned to us more than once.

Some Discernment

As I drove to the hospital on the day of the evaluation I began to wonder if there could be an evil spirit involved in this unusual state of deep sleep. I hoped that I would get there before anyone else so that I might address this in prayer over mother. I walked through the door and saw my sister Rita sitting in the room. The evaluation was only thirty minutes away. Rita had tried to wake her, but she was still asleep. I went over and sat down on the right side of the bed, and Rita was sitting on her left. I proceeded to stroke her face and hands. I touched her eyelids and tried to pry them open. I was telling her she had to wake up, and how important it was. Nothing I did helped. Rita said she and a nurse had already done all these things before I got there. My mind was racing. The clock was ticking, and I knew it was just a matter of minutes before the nurse would arrive. The hospital would dismiss her, but we had no place for her to go. I looked at Rita and then leaned over, touched Mother, and whispered, "I bind you spirit of coma and death in the name of Jesus." The instant I said this her eyes popped wide open. Rita and I looked at each other in amazement. It was so dramatic we had no doubt at all what had just happened. Not only did she open her eyes, she smiled at us and tried to talk. We were joyous.

The Evaluation

A few minutes later the nurse arrived and the evaluation began. She sat mother up in a chair and talked to her. Mother tried to cooperate, which she had not been doing previously. She smiled and tried to talk. The woman was impressed and said they could definitely work with her. She stated that she would recommend this to the insurance company. Yes! She could be rehabilitated! We literally jumped for joy. There was hope for her. Mother was then helped back to bed. The minute the woman left, Mother's eyes were closed again. She was back in her sleepy state and not responding at all. It was incredible. Rita and I knew that God had answered our prayers and had come through for us. I was quietly thanking and praising God. I was grateful that Jesus had given us authority over demons (Mark 16:17). He was so good and was taking care of Mother's and our needs. What a wonderful, caring God we have. The awesome power of prayer was amply demonstrated. The hospital chaplain, a Catholic priest, gave Mother the sacrament of the anointing of the sick with oil (James 5:13–15), which Mother wanted.

Mother was transferred to the skilled nursing center, where we hoped that she could be helped. We knew we could not send her back to her apartment like this, although that is the only place she wanted to be. She asked us constantly to take her home. We encouraged her to cooperate. We did not want her to spend the rest of her life in this condition. They were not sedating her now, because they were trying to work with her. She did not want to eat or do any of the physical therapy. We all could see the emotional and physical suffering. As the days passed, it was clear that she was not able to do the necessary work to recover. It was all too much for her. As Mother's suffering increased, the family agreed she needed to be sedated enough to ease her pain.

The condition I found Mother in the night before she died was very disturbing. She had two aides working with her. She was in what looked like an unconscious state. I wondered if death was near. My heart was heavy as I drove home. I prayed for God to end her suffering one way or another.

Early the next morning, December 18, 2000, the head nurse called to tell me mother was not responding. I heard myself ask if Mother was going to die today, and she said Mother did not have any signs of imminent death. Rita was supposed to meet me at the nurses' center

Divine Help at My Mother's Death

at 9:45 A.M. so we could talk to Mother's doctor about Hospice Care. I thought she might not make it through the week.

Death Comes Quickly and Peacefully

I left home for the nursing center, and grabbed my Bible on the way out. This was the first day I had taken it, but I felt the need to have it with me. I entered Mother's room around 9:40 A.M., and there were three people around the bed working with her. The head nurse looked up and said, "This is going much faster than we thought." It looked like Mother had just had a bath. Her hair was wet, and they were combing it. They had mother on her side facing the chair in which I would sit. Another aide was putting blush and lipstick on her, which they had never done before. They pulled the curtain around the bed on both sides for more privacy in her two-person room. The aide returned and put a blue afghan over the top of mother's hospital bedspread, another thing they had never done before. Even though they did not say anything to me about Mother dying, it was evident that they knew she would. Many confusing thoughts were going through my mind. I decided I would not leave her side, but I had no idea death would come so quickly.

Her eyes were open, and she looked so different with her wet curly hair. Mother had always been a very beautiful woman even in her old age; but these last two weeks had taken a toll. Her face looked so thin. She was not making a sound. I felt she could hear me when I spoke, but I was not sure she could see me even though her eyes were open. She was perfectly still.

I glanced at the door repeatedly, expecting Rita to arrive any minute. After about fifteen or twenty minutes, I began to feel that Mother might be dying very soon.

All during this time I was praying out loud and talking to Mother. I opened my Bible and read a few Psalms and scriptures from Song of Solomon and put Mother's name in the scriptures. I said the Lord's Prayer out loud and leaned over and whispered in Mother's ear an "act of contrition," which is a repentance prayer. I knew she would want

95

that. I named all of her children, and after each name, I would tell her how much they loved her. I told her that she was a wonderful mother and how much we all loved her. I told her that Dad and Paul and her parents were waiting for her, and that she would see them all soon. I told her how much Jesus loved her, and that He was waiting for her. I told her the angels were going to come and take her to heaven. I put my hand on the top of her head while I prayed and praised God. I noticed heat was surrounding my hand and the top of her head. I felt it was the presence of the Holy Spirit.

I realized death was very near. After a few minutes, I leaned over mother and whispered in her ear, "Mother, we all release you to go to heaven in the name of Jesus." I looked at my watch; it was 10:10 a.m. As I watched her, I knew she was not going to breathe again, and she never did take another breath. I felt she was gone, but I just sat with her for another five minutes. When the aide stuck her head in, I asked her to get the nurse to check her vital signs. I told her I believed Mother was gone. Three of them rushed in and checked her pulse and nodded to me that she was gone. They were stunned that she had died so quickly. They said they were really fooled. I knew God, in His mercy, had taken her quickly. It was very peaceful. After a few minutes Rita walked in. I then called Joe and the family. We called the funeral home and waited by mother's bedside for them to arrive. We all watched as they took her out the front door in the snow. It was finally over. Mother was out of her pain, and, in spite of my sadness, I was grateful and filled with peace and relief that she was no longer suffering. She never had to move to a nursing home to live, which was an answer to our prayers. She was only there for one week—to die.

CHAPTER 15

ISRAEL AND THE TRUMAN CONNECTION

The Blessings of Abraham

Many times I marveled at the number of healings some of my family members had received since becoming involved in Mike Bickle's ministry. Besides the healings of Joe, Terri, Rita, and myself, there have been others. The extended family has had, to date, a total of nine healings since seeking the ministry of Mike Bickle, either at the church when he was pastor or later when he became Director of the International House of Prayer of Kansas City.

The reason for this unusually large number of healings has gradually emerged. I believe there is a spiritual connection between these family blessings in the present generation and the presidency of Harry S. Truman, because of his role in establishing God's purposes for the new state of Israel in 1948. In November 2002, Mike Bickle also revealed a prophetic connection of his own to Harry Truman and to Israel.

Truman Recognizes Israel

In 1999 I read Rick Joyner's, *The Harvest*, in which he talked about the blessings of Abraham.[1] The Bible says that those who bless Israel will be blessed, as will their seed. (See Genesis 12:2–3). Joyner said:

> For example, it was because of one righteous act by Harry
> S. Truman, when he recognized the new state of Israel
> against the counsel of almost everyone in his government as
> well as world opinion, his home state of Missouri will be

97

favored as a center of revival in the U.S., and his home town of Independence, MO (Kansas City area) will become a blessing to many other nations.

Harry Truman—A Man of Faith

Some have said that my Uncle Harry recognized Israel for political reasons, but that is not true. He recognized Israel because he believed it was in America's national interest and because he knew what the Bible said about Israel and the Jewish people. Uncle Harry had read the Bible from cover to cover three times by the time he was thirteen or fourteen years old.[2] He continued to study and read it throughout his life.

William Hillman writes in *Mr. President*, "I asked the President what books had influenced him the most and he replied, 'The one that had the most influence is right here—the Holy Bible.'"[3] He told Hillman, "Of course, the Sermon on the Mount is the greatest of all things in the Bible, a way of life, and maybe some day men will get to understand it as the real way of life." He also wrote, "The fundamental basis of this nation's law was given to Moses on the Mount."

Uncle Harry also gave Hillman a copy of a prayer that he prayed his whole life. The handwritten note that accompanied the prayer said:

"This prayer...has been said by me—by Harry S. Truman—from high school days, as window washer, bottle duster, floor scrubber in an Independence, Mo., drugstore, as a timekeeper on a railroad contract gang, as an employee of a newspaper, as a bank clerk, as a farmer riding a gang plow behind four horses and mules, as a fraternity official learning to say nothing at all if good could not be said of a man, as a public official judging the weaknesses and shortcomings of constituents, and as President of the United States of America."

The Personal, Lifelong Prayer of Harry S. Truman

Oh! Almighty and Everlasting God, Creator of Heaven, Earth and the Universe:
Help me to be, to think, to act what is right, because

*it is right; make me truthful, honest, and honorable in
all things; make me intellectually honest for the sake
of right and honor and without thought of reward to
me. Give me the ability to be charitable, forgiving,
and patient with my fellowmen—help me to understand their motives and their shortcomings even as
Thou understandest mine!*
Amen, Amen, Amen.

Uncle Harry's diary entry on June 1, 1952, showed that not only
did he pray, but he also had the faith to believe God heard his prayers
and would guide him. Here is a portion of his entry where he wrote
about how Jesus had come into the world to teach sinners how to
approach His Father "...The way is direct and straight. Any man can
tell the Almighty and Most Merciful God his troubles and directly ask
for guidance. *He will get it.*" [4]

Truman Helps Fulfill Biblical Prophecy

The dispersion, or scattering, of the Israelites from the land of Israel
throughout the world was prophesied in the Old Testament. Their
regathering and return to their land was also specifically predicted.
Appendix A, Biblical Prophecies About the Restoration of Israel, dis-
cusses some of the prophecies of the book of Ezekiel concerning Israel,
and shows that the reestablishment of the state of Israel in 1948 was a
fulfillment of Ezekiel 36, which was prophesied over two thousand five
hundred years ago.

Michael T. Benson, author of *Harry S. Truman and the Founding of
Israel,* states that Truman "was heavily influenced by a biblical
upbringing well-larded with Judeo-Christian themes and by a Baptist
training that stressed a Jewish return to Zion. Truman's favorite Psalm,
number 137, is illustrative of this background: 'By the rivers of
Babylon, there we sat down, yea, we wept, when we remembered
Zion.'" [5] The Psalm speaks of the exile of the Israelites in Babylon after
King Nebuchadnezzar conquered Israel, razed Jerusalem, and led

much of the population into captivity in Babylon. Benson also stated that Truman "insisted the Old Testament had made a commitment to the Jewish people that someday they would have a homeland of their own." Uncle Harry knew the Jewish race was God's chosen people and he wanted to do the right thing. He said in a letter to Eleanor Roosevelt in August 1947 that his sympathy had always been on their side.[6]

Margaret Truman wrote of her father's recognition of Israel in 1948 in her book, *Harry S. Truman*:[7]

> On May 14, Israel declared itself a state. Eleven minutes later [Press Secretary] Charlie Ross issued a statement announcing a de facto recognition of Israel by the government of the United States. This was a decision made by Dad alone, in spite of the opposition of the State Department conspirators who for a time even had Secretary of State Marshall convinced that recognition should be withheld.

War came after Israel came into being. In *The Man From Missouri* Alfred Steinberg writes:[8]

> The aftermath was, of course, war between the Arabs and Jews. But the new nation held its own. A year later, the Chief Rabbi of Israel... wanted to meet Truman and thank him. [Dave] Niles recalled: "Rabbi Herzog told Truman, 'God put you in your mother's womb so you would be the instrument to bring about the rebirth of Israel after two thousand years.' I thought he was overdoing things, but when I looked over at the President, tears were running down his cheeks."

God Keeps His Word

After reading Rick Joyner's book, I asked Mike Bickle if he thought our family's healings (blessings) were somehow connected to Uncle Harry recognizing Israel. Mike said yes, he definitely believed they were connected.

God's Word is true and in the Bible God promised to bless those who blessed Israel, and He further declared that He would bless their seed down through the generations. I believe that some of the Truman family members and their spouses are receiving healings and blessings down through the generations like the Scriptures promise, because our Uncle Harry, over much opposition, recognized Israel, and this pleased the Lord.

Mike Bickle's Prophetic Connection to Truman

In November 2002 Mike presented a series of twelve seminars that focused on the prophetic history of his ministry.[9] In one session, he revealed a connection of his own with Harry Truman. It was the reason he moved his church on June 1, 1985 from Overland park, Kansas, to Grandview, Missouri, just a few blocks from the Truman farm on Blue Ridge Boulevard.

Mike Bickle stated that on March 7, 1983 Bob Jones, the prophetic voice of Shepherd's Rod Ministry, gave him a prophetic word from the Lord. Among other things, Mike said that Bob Jones prophesied that Mike would lead a worldwide youth prayer movement and that his ministry would be like that of Harry S. Truman. He said that Jones believed that Truman, whether he realized it or not, was an intercessor for Israel when he recognized her as a new state in 1948. Truman's support was the most significant vote for Israel to become a nation. Mike further revealed that Bob Jones said that God appointed and used Harry Truman (just as Rabbi Herzog said). According to Jones' prophecy, Mike's ministry would rally young people in prayer for the birthing of revival in Israel.

Prophecy Comes True

Mike also stated that Bob Jones told him that, as a prophetic token, God was going to move his church from Overland Park, Kansas, to a Grandview location near Harry Truman's farm home. Two years later, in 1985, Mike Bickle found himself moving his church to Grandview to a worship center close to the old Truman farm home, which is now a museum, and the land that Harry Truman farmed as a young man. Mike had forgotten about the prophecy until Bob Jones reminded him *after* the church had moved.

Harry S. Truman by the front porch of the family farmhouse in Grandview, with his mother, Martha Truman, and his grandmother, Harriet Louise Young. The photo is believed to date between 1906 and 1909. The house is about 300 yards from the church that Mike Bickle established in 1985.

Praying for Israel

On January 26, 2003 Mike Bickle knew it was time to start the God-given Israel mandate that he had carried in his heart for twenty years. This is now one of the important focuses of the International House of Prayer—praying for Israel. It is a worship movement with prayer and fasting particularly for revival in Israel.

The Israel Connection

I realize now that in 1997 the Holy Spirit led me, not to a *church*, but to Mike Bickle's *ministry*. Israel is the centerpiece of our connection. Consider the following relationships:

☩ Harry Truman helped fulfill Biblical prophecy by recognizing Israel in 1948.

☩ Bob Jones prophesied that Mike Bickle's ministry

would focus on prayer for revival in Israel and would move his church near Truman's farm home.

☦ Harry Truman's family members associated with Mike Bickle's ministry have been blessed with healings.

☦ Rick Joyner prophesied that the Kansas City area would be favored as a center of revival because of Harry Truman's recognition of Israel.

The Lord still loves His people Israel, and He has used Harry S. Truman, Mike Bickle, Bob Jones, and various Truman family members to bring about and to demonstrate His purposes for Israel.

That is why the International House of Prayer in Kansas City is an important part of my life now. This is where the Lord wants me to be, as well as Joe and Rita. Because one of the main focuses of Mike's ministry is praying for Israel, and the Lord has also impressed upon me to pray for Israel, I now know the Lord has joined us together in prayer for this purpose. We are privileged to be a part of this ministry and all of its history. God is full of delightful surprises!

Pray for the peace of Jerusalem: May they prosper who love you. Peace be within your walls. Prosperity within your palaces.

—PSALM 122:6–7, NKJV

And the LORD will take possession of Judah as His inheritance in the Holy Land, and will again choose Jerusalem.

—ZECHARIAH 2:12, NKJV

Oh, that the salvation of Israel would come out of Zion! When the LORD brings back the captivity of His people, Let Jacob rejoice and Israel be glad.

—PSALM 14:7

For thus says the LORD of hosts: He sent Me after glory, to the nations which plunder you; for he who touches you [Israel] touches the apple of His eye.

—ZECHARIAH 2:8, NKJV

But Judah shall abide forever, and Jerusalem from generation to generation.

—JOEL 3:20, NKJV

Statement of President Harry. S. Truman recognizing Israel on May 14, 1948. The corrections, signature, and date are his handwriting (from the Truman Library and Museum).

CHAPTER 16

GOD CONTINUES TO MOVE

J oe and I are now in wonderful unity and attend the same church once again. The Holy Spirit has taken us both to a new place, a special non-denominational, charismatic church with a healing ministry, where we can worship together. This is a beautiful blessing from the Lord.

We regularly spend time at *The International House of Prayer of Kansas City* (IHOP) where Mike Bickle is the director. After pastoring for twenty-five years, Mike resigned as Senior Pastor of Metro Christian Fellowship and in May 1999 started IHOP-KC. This organization is committed to prayer, intercession, worship, healing, and prophesying; fasting covering three hundred sixty-five days a year; and the Great Commission, proclaiming Jesus to all nations (Mark 16:15). The work includes equipping and sending missionaries as dedicated intercessors and evangelists working for revival in the Church and a great harvest among the lost (Rev. 14:14–16).

Christians, regardless of denomination, who believe in the Bible, and that Jesus is their Lord and Savior, come from all over the United States and the world to worship and to intercede in prayer together. In June 2000 eight Catholic representatives from Italy visited the House of Prayer for ten days. The group included Salvatore Martinez, the director of the Catholic Charismatic Renewal in Italy. Salvatore said we should point our fingers at Jesus and not at each other. He said the greatest wish of Jesus is that we are united. This group had a real desire for unity in the body of Christ. There was an exchange of ideas and teachings, with love and respect among all. We are seeing a heart for unity in the body of Christ.

James Patrick Keleher, the Catholic Archbishop of Kansas City met with Mike Bickle and other leaders and said in a letter dated February 28, 2001, to church Mission Friends:

> The International House of Prayer in Kansas City, MO, is active in prayer and reflection twenty-four hours a day, seven days a week. I have met with the leaders of this group, and am impressed with their sincerity and good will…I find this House of Prayer vision to be a blessing to the Catholic Church, and am grateful to hear of the love and increasingly fruitful dialogue that is taking place there.

He also spoke of this "ecumenical house of prayer that is seeking to move toward Christian unity and to healing the wounds of division through prayer and good works."

Prayers set to live music are offered to God twenty-four hours a day, seven days a week at the House of Prayer. We feel privileged that we can be a part of this.

A healing ministry began on September 19, 2002. Joe, Rita, and I are involved in this ministry, where we have the joy of praying for people and seeing them healed.

Through our desire for continued spiritual growth, we attend Bible classes, seminars, and numerous Christian group gatherings where all are seeking intimacy with God, the gifts of the Spirit, and praying for the sick. We have witnessed many healings, deliverances, and miracles. Here is an example of just one miracle we have seen at a group meeting. One night, a woman came for prayer who was blind in one eye because of a brain tumor. After hands-on prayer, 80 percent of her sight was restored. Her doctor confirmed this. The next week she came back for more prayer, and her eyesight was completely recovered. Again, her doctor confirmed the healing and could find no evidence of the brain tumor. This was an awesome miracle that we witnessed. We have seen ears opened, eyes healed, backs healed, victory over terminal diseases, and much more.

I counseled a woman whose sister had recently died of breast cancer and she herself had large, painful breast tumors. After she received the

God Continues to Move

information on healing that I sent her, she and her husband prayed and put the Bible principles into practice. She later wrote me that she was healed overnight, and the breast cysts were gone! They rejoiced in the Lord. I was blessed to be a part of this awesome miracle.

I know God heals today! I used to believe that a miraculous healing was something very rare, reserved only for the most pious and saintly. But I now know many people who have been healed of serious, incurable diseases as well as minor illnesses. But if you do not believe in healing, you probably will not receive it. For God honors faith (Heb. 11:6). The healing ministries, as well as many individual Christians, seek, have faith in, and receive awesome healings.

Jesus, just before He ascended into Heaven, said one of the signs of believers would be "they will lay hands on the sick, and they will recover" (Mark 16:18, NKJV). James 5:13–15 prescribes the anointing of the sick with oil by the elders of the church, and states that through their prayer of faith the Lord will save, "heal", the sick person and raise him up. All Christians must begin to appropriate this authority over sickness that the Lord has given us. Miracles of healing are a testimony to unbelievers of the power of the God we serve, and will help spread the gospel around the world, fulfilling the commission Jesus gave us:

> And He said to them, 'Go into all the world and preach the gospel to every creature. He who believes and is baptized will be saved; but he who does not believe will be condemned. And these signs will follow those who believe: In My name they will cast out demons; they will speak with new tongues; they will take up serpents; and if they drink anything deadly, it will by no means hurt them; they will lay hands on the sick, and they will recover.'
>
> —MARK 16:15–18, NKJV

PART III

BIBLE PRINCIPLES
AFFECTING HEALING

CHAPTER 17

KNOWLEDGE NEEDED
FOR HEALING:
IMPORTANT BIBLE TRUTHS

God

God is still speaking to people today as he did to the prophets in the Old Testament (Heb. 13:8). Men prophesied in the Old Testament, they prophesied in the early church, and they are still prophesying today.[1] This was quite a stunning revelation to me. (See Acts 2:17; John 16:15).

The Bible

The Bible is the living Word of God inspired by the Holy Spirit (2 Tim. 3:16–17; 2 Pet. 1:20–21). The Word is as true today as it was when it was first written. The Bible is God speaking to us. When we approach the Scriptures in faith, the Holy Spirit will guide us. He is our teacher (John 14:26). There is supernatural healing power in the spoken Word of God. It is medicine to our body and soul (Prov. 4:20–22). We must feed our spirit, and we do that by reading God's Word. Holy Scripture, when believed and spoken, promotes healing, deliverance, and also covers circumstances in our lives, causing them to change. It is alive and full of power. Hebrews 4:12 says, "For the word of God is quick, and powerful, and sharper than any two edged sword, piercing even to the dividing asunder of soul and spirit, and of the joints and marrow, and is a discerner of the thoughts and intents of the heart."

The Bible is God's blueprint for living our lives in victory. We need to believe what God says in His Word. He says what He means and He means what He says!

Purgatory

I now believe that purgatory does not exist. It is not mentioned in Scripture, and the concept conflicts with the all-sufficient nature of Jesus' sacrifice on the cross as stated, for example, in Hebrews 7:27.

Salvation

You hear people say there are many ways to God, but that is another deception from the world. The Bible says there is only one way to salvation and that is through faith in Jesus Christ as Lord and Savior. Jesus himself said in Mark 16:16, referring to preaching the gospel, "He who believes and is baptized will be saved; but he who does not believe will be condemned." Acts 4:12, "Nor is there salvation in any other name [other than Jesus] under heaven given among men by which we must be saved." 1 John 2:22–23 states, "Who is a liar but he who denies that Jesus is the Christ? He is antichrist who denies the Father and the Son. Whoever denies the Son does not have the Father either; he who acknowledges the Son has the Father also" (NKJV).

Salvation is not about converting people to a religion. It is about bringing people to the knowledge, love, and acceptance in their hearts of Jesus Christ. (See Matthew 10:33; Romans 1:16; 2 Timothy 3:15.)

Prayer Power

The only person to pray to is God. I used to pray to Mary, the mother of Jesus, and the saints to intercede for me with God, because that is what I had been taught. It was not until I read in the Scriptures what Jesus had to say about this matter that I learned how to pray correctly. Jesus told us to pray to the Father. When the apostles asked Him how to pray, he began the Lord's Prayer by addressing our Father (Luke 11:2, Matt. 6:9). God wants an intimate relationship with us with no one in between. I was glad the misconception that I had been under for years was revealed. The following are Bible truths concerning this (NKJV):

In John 14:6 Jesus said, "I am the way, the truth, and the life. *No one comes to the Father except through Me.*" The Bible states in 1 Timothy 2:5, "For there is one God and *one Mediator between God and men, the Man Christ Jesus.*" This scripture clearly states that only Jesus intercedes for us to the Father. Finally, Hebrews 7:25 says, "Therefore He is also able to save to the uttermost *those who come to God through Him,* since *He [Jesus] always lives to make intercession for them*" (emphasis added in above verses).

Gifts of the Spirit

The Holy Spirit gives Christians spiritual gifts. Nine gifts are listed in Scripture: the word of wisdom, word of knowledge, faith, gifts of healing, working of miracles, prophecy, discerning of spirits, tongues, and interpretation of tongues, distributed to us individually as the Spirit wills (1 Cor. 12:7–11).

The Leading and Teaching of the Holy Spirit

Many people talk about following *their* "inner voice." They do not know that the voice they are hearing is the Holy Spirit. I was taught that I was the temple of the Holy Spirit, but that is as far as it went. I was not taught that the Holy Spirit leads us. After giving my life to Jesus, I learned through my own experience, and reading the Bible, that the Holy Spirit teaches and leads us. In John 14:26 Jesus says, "But the Comforter, which is the Holy Ghost, whom the Father will send in my name, he shall teach you all things, and bring all things to your remembrance, whatsoever I have said unto you."

Fr. Thomas Dubay in *Fire Within* writes: "Jesus promised the apostles that the Advocate, the Holy Spirit, would come and teach them everything that He Himself had taught. This Spirit of Truth was to speak to them and lead them to 'the complete truth' (John 16:13). Jesus

Knowledge Needed for Healing

explicitly promised this would go on 'forever,' and therefore we rightly expect the faithful to be enlightened from within throughout all the ages (John 14:15–17). His [the Lord's] communications are heard by the humble and the obedient. Scripture takes it for granted that God intervenes in the affairs of men."[2]

The Cross and Healing

Jesus not only died for our sins, but He also died for our sickness and disease. As Isaiah 53:4–5 states, "And by His stripes [wounds] we are healed." He took our infirmities and bore our sicknesses (Matt. 8:17). The Scripture says disease is a curse (Deuteronomy 28:58–61) and Jesus became a curse and took that curse on the Cross (Gal. 3:13).

Sickness, disease, and early death are not God's will for us. God wants us healed, delivered, and set free, but there are things we have to do. Jesus died for forgiveness of our sins, but we must repent of sin and forgive others to receive that forgiveness.

Jesus died for the healing of our diseases, but we must become sanctified and seek the healing He won for us two thousand years ago. Many of us were taught that Jesus died for our sins, but that is only half of the truth. The Bible clearly states that Jesus died for our sins *and* our infirmities. We must believe in healing as we believe in the forgiveness of sin. We must believe it, seek it, and receive it. **Appendix B**, Seeking Divine Healing, shows eighteen ways to receive healing from God.

Spiritual Roots and Blocks

There are often spiritual blocks to healing and spiritual roots to many diseases. Of course, God can heal as He pleases, but many times spiritual blocks and roots must be addressed before healing can occur.[3] **Appendix C**, Spiritual Roots of Disease, lists forty-seven roots with nine specific examples. **Appendix D**, Spiritual Blocks to Healing, shows thirty-two blocks that can hinder healing.

Evil Spirits and Disease

Evil spirits can play a role in sickness and disease. Some illnesses cannot heal until the oppression of an evil spirit has been removed through deliverance *in the name of Jesus*.[4,5] I have witnessed deliverance and healing many times through the power of the Holy Spirit. All the healings of asthma I have seen involved deliverance from a spirit of infirmity or a spirit of fear. It has been estimated that about one-third of Jesus' healings involved casting out evil spirits. For example, Matthew 17:18, "And Jesus rebuked the devil [demon]; and he departed out of him; and the child was cured from that very hour." (Also see Acts 10:38.)

Keeping Your Healing

Matthew 13:19 says, "When anyone hears the word of the kingdom, and does not understand it, then the wicked one comes and snatches away what was sown in his heart. This is he who received seed by the wayside" (NKJV). When we are being healed, or have been prayed for and received our healing, we must stand firm against any symptoms that try to come upon us. The demons can bring the symptoms of our sickness again to try and convince us that we were not really healed. The devil is a liar (John 8:44) and wants us to look at our symptoms, which will cause unbelief and doubt to enter our mind. We must stand against this and focus on God's promises and the healing we received. Speak out God's Scriptures concerning this. God's Word has to take root in our heart.

The Power of the Tongue

Death and life are in the power of the tongue...

—PROVERBS 18:21

Every negative word spoken has a detrimental effect on your life and your health. Every positive word spoken has power and promotes well-being. We get what we say. I have seen this work in my own life. You can live in defeat or victory. In Mark 11:23 Jesus said, "For assuredly, I say to you, whoever says to this mountain [your problem/sickness], 'Be removed and be cast into the sea,' and does not doubt in his heart, but *believes* that those things he says will be done, *he will have whatever he says*. Therefore I say to you, whatever things you ask when you pray, believe that you receive them, and you will have them" (NKJV, emphasis added). Do not talk sickness, doubt, and unbelief. Continually speak what you need (according to the Scriptures), and faith and victory will be released.[6] See **Appendix F**, Healing Scriptures and God's Promises.

Sin

Sin encompasses more than breaking the Ten Commandments (see **Appendix E**, Sin: A Block to Healing, which lists sixty-nine sins revealed in the Bible). God's Word tells us that we receive blessings when we keep the Word of God, His commandments and His statutes, and curses, sickness, and death when we do not (Deut. 28). God's desire is to bless us, but He will not violate our free will. If we choose the things He has forbidden then we will bring trouble into our lives and block His hand from bestowing the blessings He has for us (Deut. 28:15).

> I call heaven and earth to record this day against you, that I have set before you life and death, blessing and cursing: therefore choose life, that both thou and thy seed (descendants) may live
>
> — DEUTERONOMY 30:19

Entertainment

Horror movies and videos, including books and games, can open the door to spirits of fear (2 Tim. 1:7) and nightmares. I know of very small children who have needed prayer and ministry because of this. Sometimes a spirit of fear has to be cast out before the child is at peace again. Many parents do not realize the importance of protecting their children of all ages from this kind of "entertainment." Adults would also be wise to abstain.

Occultic "Art" and Superstitions

There are people who have items of superstition or of the occult (astrological symbols, good luck charms, Ouija boards, to name a few) and images of false gods (sun gods, Buddhas, etc.) in their possession, and they think it is all right. They mistakenly think that it is "art." Because they do not believe in the idol as an item of the occult, or the underlying practices, they feel it is acceptable to have such items. Lacking knowledge, many well-meaning people buy, own and collect items such as these. This attitude opens the door for occult evil spirits to legally enter a person's life. They can bring sickness and disease. I have witnessed this in ministry. With repentance, including the removal and destruction of such objects, I have also witnessed healing, deliverance, and victory.

> You shall burn the carved images of their gods with fire; you shall not covet the silver or gold that is on them, nor take it for yourselves, lest you be snared by it; for it is an abomination to the LORD your God. Nor shall you bring an abomination into your house, lest you be doomed to destruction like it. You shall utterly detest it and utterly abhor it, for it is an accursed thing.
>
> —DEUTERONOMY 7:25–26, NKJV

Keeping these things not only breaks the First Commandment, but is also an abomination before God and can definitely be a block to healing. No *thing* is worth that. Giving such items a place of honor in the home, or business, or even in a museum is an affront to God and He Himself tells us that it is an abomination to Him. (See also Deut. 12:1–4; 5:6–10; Isa. 2:6–22; Isa. 45:16, 20; Jer. 51:17–18.)

A FEW EXAMPLES OF COMMON OCCULT ART, FALSE GODS, AND SUPERSTITIONS: THESE CAN BE BLOCKS TO HEALING

Buddha

Siddhartha Gautama, commonly known as the Buddha, founded Buddhism in the sixth century B.C. in India and Nepal. The word Buddha means "supreme enlightened one." Buddhism accepts the pan-Indian presupposition of *samsara*, in which living beings are trapped in a continual cycle of birth and death, with the momentum to rebirth provided by one's previous physical and mental actions (*karma*). The release from this cycle of rebirth and suffering is the total transcendence called *nirvana*. Unfortunately, some people use Buddha statues and art work as decor in offices and homes.[1]

Cupid

In Roman mythology, Cupid was the son of Venus, the goddess of love. In Greek mythology, he was known as Eros, the son of Aphrodite. He is commonly represented as a mischievous, winged, naked, infant boy with a bow and arrows. It was believed that the arrows would pierce the hearts of his victims, causing them to fall deeply in love. Cupid is a common symbol of Valentines Day.[2]

117

Gargoyles

First appearing in the 1200s, they are grotesque carvings originally designed as ornamental waterspouts. They are seen on medieval churches and cathedrals. The gargoyle myth holds that the gargoyle serves as protector and will ward off any evil that may attempt to corrupt the dwelling. They can stand guard and ward off unwanted spirits and other creatures. The belief is that they come alive at night when everyone is asleep so they can protect you when you are vulnerable. Modern-day gargoyles have been used as Gothic ornaments, icons of mythology, and cartoon heroes.[3]

Kokopelli

This southwestern American Indian deity is thought to represent fertility and the untamed energy of nature. This ancient flute player is believed to be one of the oldest of the supernatural figures of Amerindian myth. The figure is portrayed on Indian jewelry, pottery, and fabrics. Kokopelli's likeness varies almost as much as the legends about him, but he is generally depicted as a hunchbacked flute player in a dancing pose.[4]

Fairy

The fairy is usually depicted in folklore and legend as a diminutive supernatural being, in human shape, clever and mischievous, with magical powers. It is known by many names and in many forms: brownie, dwarf, elf, gnome, goblin, leprechaun, and pixie.[5]

Dragon

A dragon is a legendary reptilian monster similar in form to a crocodile but with wings, huge claws, and fiery breath. The dragon symbol has been used in a number of ways and beliefs: a symbol for destruction and evil, the ability to understand and teach mortals the secrets of

A Few Examples...

the earth, a symbol of sovereignty, and symbol of good fortune.[6] In the Book of Job, 41:1–34, there is a good description of the dragon known as Leviathan, a representation of evil and of Satan. The dragon of Revelation 12 is clearly a representation of Satan.

Sun Gods

Many cultures use different images to worship the sun as a god. Today you see the sun god represented on an array of objects including fabrics, art, and household items. The image shows the sun with a face and rays flowing out in all directions.[7]

Unicorn

This mythological animal resembled a horse but had a single horn set in the middle of its forehead. The horn was believed to have magical powers.[8]

Anyone possessing these or similar items ought to repent and destroy them. These objects are an abomination before God and can be a block to healing.

> You shall burn the carved images of their gods with fire; you shall not covet the silver or gold that is on them, nor take it for yourselves, lest you be snared by it; for it is an abomination to the LORD your God. Nor shall you bring an abomination into your house, lest you be doomed to destruction like it. You shall utterly detest it and utterly abhor it, for it is an accursed thing.
>
> —DEUTERONOMY 7:25–26, NKJV

119

APPENDICES

BIBLICAL PROPHECIES ABOUT THE RESTORATION OF ISRAEL

BY JOSEPH P. GRACEY

Summary

Chapter 15 demonstrated that, when President Harry S. Truman immediately extended the recognition of the United States to the fledgling state of Israel on May 14, 1948, he knew what he was doing. He was a knowledgeable Christian who was familiar with the Bible and its prophecies about the reestablishment of Israel. When Chief Rabbi Herzog of Israel told him that the Lord put him in his mother's womb so that he could fulfill his part in the Jewish regathering, his tears showed that he knew the truth of that statement.

This appendix shows that, beginning with subjugation to Babylon in 606 B.C., the Lord brought severe punishment upon His people for their sins, particularly for idolatry. This punishment continued through the destruction of the temple and Jerusalem and exile of most of the population. The Lord foresaw that Israel would not repent after the 70 years of Babylonian captivity prophesied by Jeremiah, so He decreed a total punishment of 430 years through the prophet Ezekiel. At the end of this period, the Maccabean revolution restored a semblance of independence to Israel for about a century, but, because the repentance the Lord expected never occurred, He multiplied the punishment by seven according to Leviticus 26.

In 63 B.C. the Romans ended Israel's brief independence. They put down a rebellion in 70 A.D. in which many were slaughtered, the temple was destroyed, and much of the population was sent into exile again, fulfilling the prophecies of Jesus (Matt. 24:2; Luke 21:24). After

Appendix A

the Roman occupation began, the land of Israel was ruled by external forces for more than two thousand years as the population was scattered over the whole earth.

When, with the help of Harry Truman and the United States, Israel once again became an independent nation in 1948, it was the beginning of the fulfillment of Ezekiel 36 and Ezekiel 39:21–29, which speak of the end time restoration of God's people to their land. The exact time of that restoration (May of 1948) was prophesied in Ezekiel 4 (combined with Leviticus 26) more than 2,500 years before it happened. The Lord indeed still rules and is in control of human history.

The details supporting the truth of this summary are shown below.

Israel's Rebirth in 1948

Chapter 15 outlines part of the immediate historical context of the reestablishment of the state of Israel on May 15, 1948. The Holocaust and worldwide persecution of Jews had created large numbers of Jewish refugees after World War II who wished to immigrate to and reclaim British-controlled "Palestine," the location of the ancient land (once called Canaan) that God had promised by covenant to Abraham, Isaac, Jacob, and their descendants (Gen. 12:7; 15:7, 18; 17:8; 24:7).

Because of the slaughter and persecution of Jews during the war, world opinion had created a favorable climate for the recreation of a Jewish state by partitioning Palestine. On November 29, 1947, the General Assembly of the United Nations voted to authorize the partition. The British government, which had been placed in charge of Palestine in 1917 under a mandate from the League of Nations, quickly stated its intention to end its stewardship of the territory as of May 15, 1948. A provisional Jewish government declared on May 14, 1948, that the new state of Israel would begin functioning the next day. When, only a few minutes after this declaration, President Harry S. Truman threw the prestige of the United States behind the Jewish government by granting de facto recognition to the state of Israel, its existence was assured.

123

The Babylonian Captivity of Israel

Some of the important Old Testament prophecies concerning the restoration of Israel in 1948 were revelations of the Lord to Ezekiel. Ezekiel was one of the Hebrew captives deported to Babylon about 597 B.C. after King Nebuchadnezzar of Babylon had conquered Israel and Judah and put down a rebellion by King Zedekiah of Judah, whom Nebuchadnezzar had installed on the throne (2 Kings 24:17–20). Ezekiel's prophecies were made in Babylon (present-day southeastern Iraq) to the other Israelites who had also been exiled there by the king of Babylon.

This Babylonian captivity was brought onto Israel by the Lord as judgment for many sins, but particularly for idolatry (Jer. 44:2–6). Jeremiah, who prophesied from Jerusalem prior to the conquest, tried to warn his countrymen of the coming calamities the Lord would bring on them, but the word of the Lord he announced was ignored, and the prophet was persecuted. Jeremiah prophesied that Nebuchadnezzar would conquer Israel and Judah, "and these nations shall serve the king of Babylon seventy years" (Jer. 25:11; see also Jer. 29:10 and 2 Chron. 36:21). The conquest and exile ended the existence of an independent Jewish state.

Did Israel Repent After 70 Years of Punishment?

The Babylonian captivity ended in 538 B.C. with a decree from Cyrus the Great, King of Persia, who had conquered Babylon a year earlier, allowing the Hebrews to return to their homeland and rebuild their temple (2 Chron. 36:22–23). A group numbering nearly 50,000, led by Sheshbazzar and Zerubbabel (Ezra 2) returned after the edict (perhaps in 537 or 536 B.C.), bringing with them many of the articles from the temple that Nebuchadnezzar had looted and carried off to Babylon. The Jewish homeland continued to be ruled as a province of the Persian Empire. Rebuilding of the temple was started, but resistance from adversaries caused the project to languish for sixteen years until about 520 B.C. (Ezra 4–6).

124

Appendix A

The Lord then raised up the prophets Haggai and Zechariah. Through them He reminded the people of their evil ways (Hag. 2:14), which caused want and poverty (Hag. 1:6) and exhorted them to repent and rebuild His house. The temple was rebuilt and dedicated in about 515 B.C. (Ezra 6:13–18), but the people still did not turn from their evil ways. About one hundred years later, the prophet Malachi spoke the word of the Lord. He listed thirty-two sins committed by God's people, including dishonoring God (Mal. 1:6), offering polluted bread to God (Mal. 1:7), marriage with heathens (Mal. 2:11), sorcery, adultery, perjury (Mal. 3:5), and robbing God of tithes and offerings (Mal. 3:8–9).[1]

The rebelliousness continued even to the time of Jesus. All of Matthew 23 is an indictment by Jesus of the Jewish religious leadership, concluding with a lament over Jerusalem, "the one who kills the prophets and stones those who are sent to her! How often I wanted to gather your children together, as a hen gathers her chicks under her wings, but you were not willing… Your house is left to you desolate" (NKJV).

Jesus prophesied the destruction of the temple (Matt. 24:2; Mark 13:2) and further dispersion of the Jews. He said, "And they will fall by the edge of the sword, and be led away captive into all nations" (Luke 21:24, NKJV). The Romans quelled a rebellion in 70 A.D. Jerusalem and the temple were destroyed, about one million were killed, 97,000 were taken captive, and "the whole race was scattered among the nations."[2]

The temple has never been rebuilt; in fact, a Moslem mosque, called the Dome of the Rock, was constructed on part of the temple site about 691 A.D. Thus, God's judgment continued on Israel during this entire period because of the continued rebellion against Him.

Ezekiel Prophesies More Punishment

In Ezekiel 4:4–6, the Lord commanded the prophet to lie on his left side, and "lay the iniquity of the house of Israel upon it" for 390 days. Then he was to lie on his right side and "bear the iniquity of the house

125

of Judah forty days." The Lord said, "I have laid on you a day for each year." Thus the prophet lay on the left side, then the right for a total of 430 days to bear the iniquity of each of the two Jewish kingdoms (Israel, the Northern Kingdom, and Judah). This prophesied 430 years of punishment for their sins. The ritual was to be performed publicly in front of a clay tablet, upon which was drawn a representation of the coming siege of Jerusalem. The exact date of the prophecy is uncertain, but it had to be between Ezekiel's exile to Babylon (597 B.C.) and the siege of Jerusalem by Nebuchadnezzar (588 B.C.). Arbitrarily selecting the year 591 B.C. and moving forward in time 430 biblical years (423.8 calendar years) brings us to the year 167 B.C., which should have been the approximate date ending the punishment.[3]

This date coincides with the beginning of the Maccabean revolt of the Jews against the Seleucid Syrian king Antiochus IV Epiphanes, who had banned Jewish religious practices and set up an image of Zeus in the temple. Many of the people, particularly the aristocracy, abandoned their heritage and joined in the pagan worship. Much of the history of this revolt is recorded in the two books of Maccabees, which have not been regarded as inspired scripture by the Jews since about the first century A.D., but are still accepted by the Catholic Church. The Protestant churches also consider the books as apocryphal (not inspired). Judas Maccabeus and his brothers, all godly men like the heroes of the book of Judges, led the successful revolt and reestablished an independent Jewish state for the only time between Nebuchadnezzar's conquest of Israel in about 606 B.C. and the regathering of Israel in 1948. During the period of relative freedom, Jewish religious leaders bickered among themselves, and several major sects emerged within Judaism—the Pharisees, the Zealots, the Sadducees, and the Essenes. The latter group remained aloof, but both the Pharisees and the Sadducees led revolts against the rulers. Unrest was widespread. Independence lasted until 63 B.C. when a Roman army under Pompey entered Jerusalem. The judgment of the Lord and punishment continued against Israel.

Appendix A

Ezekiel's Prophecy of Restoration

But God had not abandoned His people. Many Old Testament prophets spoke of restoration. Ezekiel, in chapter 36, prophesied about how the mountains of Israel, desolate and swallowed up by enemies (v. 3), the shame of the nations (v. 6), would be reinhabited by "My people Israel" (v. 8). The land would be tilled and sown and the ruins rebuilt (vv. 9–10). Because the house of Israel had defiled the land by their deeds and their idols (vv. 17–18), the Lord punished them and scattered them and "dispersed them throughout the countries" (v. 19). But, for the sake of His holy name, which Israelites had continued to profane in the nations where they went (v. 22), the Lord promised, "I will take you from among the nations, gather you out of all countries, and bring you into your own land" (v. 24). He would cleanse them (v. 25) and give them new hearts (v. 26). He would prosper the land (vv. 29–30); it would "become like the garden of Eden" (v. 35). The population would increase (v. 37).

Ezekiel continued with the prophecy of the dry bones (Ezek. 37:1–14) and the two sticks (vv. 15–28). Israel, once dead, will rise with the Spirit of the Lord in her. She will regather into one kingdom (vv. 21–23), which will not be divided again.

In chapters 38 and 39, Ezekiel spoke the word of the Lord about Gog (the Antichrist) and his allies attacking a peaceful Israel, "who dwell safely, all of them dwelling without walls, and having neither bars nor gates" (Ezek. 38:11, NKJV). God will defeat Gog and destroy his armies, and birds and beasts will feast on them (39:17–20).

In Ezekiel 39:21–29 Israel's restoration to the land is summarized. They "went into captivity for their iniquity" (v. 23) and the Lord "gave them into the hand of their enemies" (v. 24). But the Lord would restore His people. "When I have brought them back from the peoples and gathered them out of their enemies' lands, and I am hallowed in them in the sight of many nations, then they shall know that I am the Lord their God, who sent them into captivity among the nations, but also brought them back to their land, and left none of them captive any longer" (vv. 27–28, NKJV).

Ezekiel continued in chapters 40 through 48 to give a detailed description of a new temple and a new city, which would be built in the latter days. The exiles returning from the Babylonian captivity did not use these plans to rebuild the temple or the city. The temple rebuilt in 515 B.C. and enhanced later was destroyed in 70 A.D. Ezekiel's temple has never been built.

This entire section of the Book of Ezekiel (chapters 36 through 48), including the restoration of Israel as an independent, prosperous nation, speaks of End-Time events and prophecies culminating in the Second Coming. The regathering of the Jews from all parts of the world and the reestablishment of the state of Israel in 1948 began the fulfillment of Ezekiel 36.

Ezekiel's Prophecy Shows the Restoration of Israel in 1948

In his book, *The Signature of God*, author Grant Jeffery provides a remarkable insight showing how the prophecy of Ezekiel 4:4–6, which decreed 430 biblical years of punishment for Israel, led directly to the restoration of Israel in 1948.[4] The key element is recognizing a precept of the Law of Moses given in Leviticus 26. It provides further punishment for situations when the Lord chastises His people and they continue to be unrepentant. "And after all this, if you do not obey Me, then I will punish you seven times more for your sins" (Leviticus 26:18, NKJV). Under this provision of the law, nonrepentance of the people during and after the prescribed punishment of Ezekiel 4 caused the chastisement to be multiplied by seven.

Jeffery places the start of the punishment at the end of the Babylonian captivity (the spring of 536 B.C.), but subtracts the 70 years of subjugation already served from the total 430 biblical years. Thus, 360 additional biblical years of punishment must be endured. When this time is multiplied by seven, because of the nonrepentance of the people, the time is extended to 2,520 biblical years, beginning in 536 B.C. As previously discussed, biblical years of 360 days each must be converted

Appendix A

to calendar years. The number of days is 2,520 years X 360 days per year, or 907,200 days. Dividing by 365.25 calendar days per year converts biblical years to 2,483.8 calendar years. Jeffery then advances this time from 536.4 B.C., adding one year because there is no year zero (i.e., January of 1 B.C. to January of 1 A.D. is one year). This calculation (2,483.8 − 536.4 + 1) shows that the end of the multiplied punishment of Israel would occur in May of 1948 (1948.4 A.D.). The new state of Israel came into existence on May 15, 1948, in exact fulfillment of the prophecy of Ezekiel 4 combined with the prescription of Leviticus 26:18.

SEEKING DIVINE HEALING: SOME WAYS TO POSITION YOURSELF TO RECEIVE FROM GOD

This is not a formula—God heals as He pleases in many different ways.

1. Have Faith in Jesus Christ.

Accepting Jesus (being born again) as your Lord and Savior is the first step. Believe that He not only died on the cross for your sins and rose from the dead, but that he took the stripes (wounds) on His back for your sickness and diseases, and that He will heal you.

2. Repent of Sin.

Take responsibility for the sins in your life, no matter how big or how small. Confess your sins and ask God's forgiveness. If necessary, apologize to others and ask for their forgiveness.

3. Seek Sanctification.

Purge sin out of your life. Guard what you read, watch, and speak. Strive for integrity, righteousness, and holiness. Regularly attend and support a church that believes and teaches the Scriptures.

4. Forgive.

Forgive others for wrongs done to you. This is absolutely necessary for healing.

5. Take God's Medicine.

Take your medicine every day by reading God's Word, the Bible, and believing what it says. (See Proverbs 4:20–22.) Accept all of God's promises as true without doubting. It is the only truth you can always count on.

6. **Praise, Worship, and Thank God Daily.**

7. **Pray Daily. Believe and Verbalize God's Promises Aloud.**

8. **Focus on Jesus, the Healer. Do Not Focus on Your Symptoms.**

9. **Take Every Thought Captive (2 Corinthians 10:5).**

You must not think or dwell on negative thoughts.

Do not associate with people who are in unbelief while you are seeking healing. It will weaken your faith for healing. Distance yourself from people who talk negatively about health issues.

10. **Renew Your Mind From Old Thought Patterns and Wrong Beliefs.**

The way you do this is by reading and studying the Bible in your personal prayer time. Believe and meditate on what God says about healing and how to live your life.

11. **Rid Yourself of Unbelief.**

God has given each one of us a measure of faith, but unbelief and doubt can counterbalance that faith. "Lord, I believe; help my unbelief!" (Mark 9:24, NKJV). Jesus said in Matthew 17:21, "However, this kind [of unbelief] does not go out except by prayer and fasting."

12. **Deal with Fear, Stress, and Anxiety.**

Fear (belief that evil may happen) is the opposite of faith (belief in God's providence). You need to completely trust God. When you truly believe that God wants the best for you and that He will take care of you, peace will come and stress (which contributes to disease) will leave.

13. **Clean House.**

Remove from your possession anything that may be offensive to God (occultic or suggestive art work, books which promote immorality or glorify evil, violent or immoral movies and games that have occultic, violent, or sexual themes.)

14. Get Hands-on Healing Prayer From People Who Believe in Healing.

15. Study the Bible.

Study the Bible in depth. Find a good Bible class. Seek out Christian television programs that espouse practical teaching of Bible truths. (Examples: Joyce Meyer, Andrew Wommack, and Kenneth Copeland.)

16. Give to the Poor.

When we give and care for the poor (see Isaiah 58:7), it helps make the way for our healing to come forth, as we see in verses 8–9 (NKJV; see also Psalm 41:1–3):

> Then your light shall break forth like the morning, your healing shall spring forth speedily, and your righteousness shall go before you; the glory of the LORD shall be your rear guard. Then you shall call, and the LORD will answer; you shall cry, and He will say, "Here I am."

17. Laugh.

The Bible says, "A merry heart does good like medicine" (Prov.17:22, NKJV). Through various studies the medical community has also shown that laughter is healing.

18. Seek Intimacy.

Set aside quiet time each day to seek intimacy with the Lord. Dwell in the secret place of His presence. Rest in His love. This is a very important key.

Appendix C

Spiritual Roots of Disease

Pastor Henry Wright, of Pleasant Valley Ministries (a Healing Ministry), states that he had observed that, regardless of denomination or church, less than 5 percent of the people prayed for were getting healed of their diseases. Pastor Wright stated that he went before God in the early 1980s and asked Him to show him truths about disease from Scripture. "It wasn't that He [God] *could not* heal. It was that we had to become sanctified in certain areas in our lives before He *would* heal. Diseases in our lives can be the result of a separation from Him and His Word in specific areas of our lives."[1]

Pastor believes that about 80 percent of all disease has a spiritual root with various psychological and biological manifestations. Healing and things you get from God, to a degree, are conditional to your obedience. He says that the knowledge he has is not only accurate scripturally, but is also accurate medically. There have been thousands of healings through his ministry that validate this.

fear	long-term fear
stress	fear of man
anxiety	fear of rejection
dread	fear of failure
bitterness (against others)	fear of abandonment
resentment	fear concerning relationships
rejection	inner conflict and turmoil
broken heart	conflict with yourself and others
broken spirit	family conflict
hope deferred	conflict with identity
rage	mistrust
anger (with yourself and others)	insecurity

lack of self-esteem
need to be loved
self-hatred
self-rejection
self-bitterness
guilt
mental torment (from life
   circumstances)
envy
jealousy
rebellion
abandonment
lack of nurturing
   (childhood/marriage)

emotional shock
abuse (verbal, emotional,
   physical, sexual)
victimization
unresolved issues
unresolved rejection
unresolved conflict
not forgiving oneself
driven to meet expectations
   of another
codependence and false
   burden-bearing
things bothering you
   long-term

Examples of Spiritual Roots of Specific Diseases

Allergies

An allergy is a hypersensitive reaction to any antigen (any substance that produces a reaction). It is an acquired, abnormal immune response to a substance (allergen) that does not normally cause a reaction. Root: long-term *fear, anxiety,* and *stress* can destroy the immune system, causing a hypersensitive reaction. *Unresolved conflict* can also be a root cause. (For every thought that you have, conscious or unconscious, there is a nerve transmission, a secretion of a hormone, or neurotransmitter somewhere in your body to react to it.)

Arthritis (simple)

Inflammation of a joint usually accompanied by pain, swelling, and frequently, changes in structure. Root: it can involve *bitterness* and *unforgiveness* against others. This differs from osteoarthritis and other forms of arthritis. There is a different spiritual root behind each type.

134

Appendix C

Asthma

There is stiffening of the cell walls of the alveoli. This causes an entrapment of carbon dioxide and an exclusion of oxygen. Thus you have breathing problems and find yourself gasping for air. Root: *deep-rooted fear, anxiety* and *stress*. The Johns Hopkins University Research Team in 1996 conclusively proved that nothing that you breathe causes an asthmatic attack.[2] Asthma is now considered an *anxiety disorder* by the medical community. It can also be inherited.

Hyperthyroidism (Graves' Disease)

It is an over-secretion of thyroxin that produces goiters, swelling of the eyes, palpitations, and tremors. Root: *emotional shock, emotional conflict, long-term anxiety, fear* and / or *self-hatred, self-rejection,* and *guilt*.

Insomnia

It is the inability to sleep at night. Sleep is regulated by the hypothalamus gland. Root: if the hypothalamus gland senses *conflict* or *fear/anxiety/stress*, it will interfere with your peace. A result can be insomnia.

Irritable Bowel Syndrome

Root: misfiring of nerve dendrites in lining of intestine because of *anxiety, fear,* and *insecurities*.

Migraines

Rooted in *guilt*, then *fear*, *inner conflict,* and *turmoil*.

Multiple Chemical Sensitivity/Environmental Illness

The immune system is destroyed, and you become allergic to almost everything, including food, pollens, perfume, and chemicals of all kinds. Root: *broken spirit, broken heart, break up in relationship, mistrust,* and *anxiety; being injured spiritually and emotionally at some point in your life*. From studying Scripture a connection was found between the spirit of man and disease. The Word of God says that a broken spirit, or broken heart, can destroy the immune system. (See Proverbs 17:22.)

135

SPIRITUAL BLOCKS TO HEALING[1]

1. Unforgiveness

This is the number one block and the most important one. (See Matthew 6:14–15.)

2. Ignorance or Lack of Knowledge

Hosea 4:6 says, "My people are destroyed for lack of knowledge" (NKJV). (See also Isaiah 5:13.)

3. No Relationship With God According to Knowledge

You must pursue a relationship with God by talking to Him and diligently seeking Him. Converse with God about the desires, plans, and purposes of His heart, not just yours. It is fellowship with our Creator. (See Hebrews 11:6.)

4. Personal and Family Sins

Isaiah 59:1–2; Exodus 20:5; Deuteronomy 5:9; Nehemiah 9:1–2

5. Not Having Faith in God

Unbelief and doubt. (See Mark 11:22; Hebrews 11:6; Hebrews 11:1.)

6. The Need to See a Miracle

Some believe that they need to see a miracle in order to receive from God. (See John 20:28–29.)

7. Looking for Signs and Wonders

Some are chasing signs and wonders rather than seeking the Word of God. We must seek God first. (See Matthew 12:38–39.)

8. Expecting God to Heal on One's Own Terms

Sometimes we expect God to heal us on our own terms and in the way that we think it should go. A spiritual root is *pride*. (See 2 Kings 5:8-14.)

9. Looking to Man Rather Than to God

Doctors have their place, but in the area of spiritually rooted disease, they will not be able to bring forth the healing—only disease management. One of the great blocks to healing from God is to look to man as your source. (See Jeremiah 17:5, 7.)

10. Not Being Honest and Transparent

Two big reasons are fear and pride. (See Proverbs 16:18.) We must humble ourselves and confess our sins. "Confess your faults one to another...that ye may be healed" (James 5:16). (See also Proverbs 28:13.)

11. Flagrant Sin or Habitual Sin

There is a difference between temptation and falling into sin, and repenting and getting out of sin, than living habitually in it. (See Galatians 5:19–21.) Habitual, unrepented, flagrant sin (and if your heart is hardened) is a major block to God healing you and meeting you in your life.

12. Robbing God in Tithes and Offerings

We must give back to God. Everything we have belongs to Him. (See Malachi 3:8–11.)

13. Some Are Just Not Saved

They do not know Jesus or the Father. (See 2 Thessalonians 2:1.)

14. Sins of Our Parents

See 2 Samuel 12:13–14; 1 Kings 14:1–13.

15. Sometimes the Sickness Is Unto Death

1 John 5:16–17; 2 Chronicles 21:4, 12–20; 2 Kings 1:2–8; 1 Chronicles 10:13–14

16. Our Allotted Time in Life Is Fulfilled

Moses in Psalm 90 wrote that God, as a promise, established man's longevity at seventy to eighty years. (See Psalm 90:10,12; Proverbs 10:27.)

17. Looking to Symptoms and Not to the Healer

Some are waiting for the symptoms of their disease to go away before they believe. We have to keep our eyes off the symptoms and keep our eyes on the Lord our Healer. (See Proverbs 18:14; Romans 8:11.)

18. Letting Fear Enter Your Heart

Fear will quench your faith. Romans 8:15, John 14:1, John 14:27, and Romans 14:23 are God's antidote to the spirit of fear.

19. Failure to Get Away in Prayer and Fasting

There's a lack of closeness in your personal relationship with Jesus and the Father. You don't pray and fast just to receive from God—you pray and fast to meet God in relationship. It is primarily for fellowship. (See Mark 2:19–20; Matthew 17:18–21.)

20. Improper Care of the Body

You are not taking care of the temple of the Holy Spirit. You must have balance in your life. You must have proper sleep, exercise, and good nutrition. (See Philippians 2:25–30.)

21. Not Discerning the Lord's Body

Taking communion in unbelief, not realizing its true significance, and not discerning the Lord's body and blood to receive the benefits by faith. Taking communion with sin in your life, without making confession unto salvation and acknowledgment of personal needs, without judging yourself so as to escape the chastening of God. (See 1 Corinthians 11:27–31.)

22. Touching God's Anointed Leaders

Speaking against pastors, leaders in the church and their families, God's servants. (See 1 Chronicles 16:22; Psalm 105:15.)

23. Immoderate Eating

You cannot expect to walk in health if you do not drink enough water and eat the proper mixture of food—good nutrition in moderation (temperance). (See 1 Corinthians 6:19–20.)

24. Pure Unbelief

See Mark 6:4–6; Hebrews 4:1–11.

25. Failing to Keep Our Life Filled Up With God

You must keep yourself "filled up" with the knowledge of God and obedience to Him. (See John 5:14; Matthew 12:43–45.)

26. Not Resisting the Enemy

See 1 Peter 5:8–9; James 4:7–8; Deuteronomy 30:19; Isaiah 38:1–5.

27. Just Giving Up

You look at your symptoms; you look at the prognosis; you look at the word *incurable*; and you come into an agreement and acceptance of all this as the truth, rather than pursuing healing in the face of what everything in the physical realm would indicate.

28. Looking for Repeated Healings Instead of Divine Health

See 3 John 1–2.

29. Rejecting Healing in the Atonement as Part of the Covenant for Today

Not believing that healing is for today. (See 1 Peter 2:24; Isaiah 53:5; Psalm 103:3.)

30. Trying to Bypass the Penalty of the Curse

People who are looking for ways to get out of disease without dealing with the root that causes the disease. If your disease is spiritually rooted, the only way healing and wholeness will come is to deal with the spiritual root through repentance and sanctification. (See Proverbs 26:2.)

31. Murmuring and Complaining

Signs of ungratefulness—these will block God's movement in our lives. (See Numbers 12:1–15; 1 Corinthians 10:10–11; Philippians 2:14–15.)

32. Hating and Not Obeying Instruction

See Proverbs 5:11–14; Isaiah 28:8–19.

———————————— ～ ————————————

If we will keep our spirits nourished with the Word of God and keep our lives free of devastating sin and occultism and exercise wisdom in the care of our bodies, we will enjoy greater and greater measures of divine health.

—PASTOR HENRY WRIGHT

SIN: A BLOCK TO HEALING

For the eyes of the Lord are on the righteous, And His ears are open to their prayers; But the face of the Lord is against those who do evil.

—1 PETER 3:12, NKJV

Now we know that God does not hear sinners; but if anyone is a worshiper of God and does His will, He hears him.

—JOHN 9:31, NKJV

REPENTANCE is an important step to healing, and God forgives repented sin.

I [Jesus] say to you that likewise there will be more joy in heaven over one sinner who repents than over ninety-nine just persons who need no repentance.

—LUKE 15:7, NKJV

Let no one say when he is tempted, "I am tempted by God"; for God cannot be tempted by evil, nor does He Himself tempt anyone.

—JAMES 1:13, NKJV

Some of the things the Bible lists as sin

Sin	Scripture references (NKJV except where listed)
unbelief	Revelation 21:8; 1 Timothy 5:8
bitterness	Ephesians 4:31
unforgiveness	Mark 11:26; Luke 17:3–4; Luke 6:37–38
revenge	Ezekiel 25:15–16
hatred	Galatians 5:20; 1 John 3:15

Sin	Scripture references (NKJV except where listed)
wrath	Ephesians 4:26, 31; Galatians 5:20; Colossians 3:8
strife, disputes, arguments	1 Timothy 6:4
anger	Ephesians 4:31; Colossians 3:8
saying "You fool!" in anger	Matthew 5:22
provoking to wrath	Ephesians 6:4
pride, arrogance	Mark 7:22; Luke 14:11; Luke 18:14; Proverbs 8:13
swearing	Matthew 5:34
clamor (shouting)	Ephesians 4:31
slander, revilers, evil speaking, perverse mouth	Ephesians 4:29–31; Colossians 3:8; 1 Corinthians 6:10; 1 Timothy 6:4; 1 Peter 2:1; Titus 3:2; Jude 8; Proverbs 8:13
malice	1 Peter 2:1; Ephesians 4:31; Colossians 3:8
lying and false witness	Revelation 21:8; Ephesians 4:25; James 3:14–16; Matthew 15:19; Colossians 3:9
deceit	Mark 7:22; 1 Peter 2:1
foolish talking, coarse jesting	Ephesians 5:4
silly or suggestive talk	Ephesians 5:3–5, NASB, NAB
obscene language	Colossians 3:8, NAB
obscenity	Ephesians 5:3–5, NIV
impurity	Ephesians 5:3–5; Colossians 3:5, NASB
sexual immorality	1 Corinthians 6:18; Revelation 21:8; Galatians 5:20; Colossians 3:5

Appendix E

Sin	Scripture references (NKJV except where listed)
fornication	Mark 7:21; Galatians 5:19–21; Ephesians 5:3–5; 1 Corinthians 6:9–10; Matthew 15:19
adultery	Mark 7:21; 1 Corinthians 6:9; Galatians 5:19–21; Luke 18:20; Matthew 15:19
lewdness	Mark 7:22; Ezekiel 16:43; 1 Peter 4:3
lust	Matthew 5:28; 1 Peter 4:3
covetousness	Mark 7:22; Ephesians 5:5; 1 Corinthians 6:10; Colossians 3:5
murmuring	John 6:43
grumbling	James 5:9
complaining, disputing	Philippians 2:14; 1 Corinthians 10:10; 1 Timothy 6:4
judging others	Matthew 7:1–2; Luke 6:37–38; Romans 2:1–3
murder	Galatians 5:21; Mark 7:21; Matthew 15:19; Revelation 21:8
hypocrisy	1 Peter 2:1
envy	James 3:14–16; 1 Peter 2:1; Galatians 5:21; 1 Timothy 6:4
jealously	Galatians 5:20
evil thoughts	Matthew 15:19; Mark 7:21
drunkenness	Galatians 5:21; Ephesians 5:18; 1 Corinthians 6:10; 1 Peter 4:3
greed	Ephesians 5:3–5, NASB; 1 Corinthians 6:9–10, NAB; Colossians 3:5, NASB

Sin	Scripture references (NKJV except where listed)
love of money	1 Timothy 6:10
unrighteousness	1 Corinthians 6:9
self-seeking, selfish ambition	James 3:14–16; Galatians 5:20
thievery	1 Corinthians 6:10; Mark 7:22; Luke 18:20; Matthew 15:19
extortion	1 Corinthians 6:10
boasting	James 3:14–16
idle words	Matthew 12:36–37
reject authority	Jude 8; Titus 3:1
revelries	Galatians 5:21; 1 Peter 4:3
incest	Leviticus 20:17
practicing homosexuality	Leviticus 20:13; 18:22; 1 Corinthians 6:9–10
sodomy	1 Corinthians 6:9
heresy	Galatians 5:20
denying Jesus	Matthew 10:32–33; Luke 10:16; Luke 12:8–9; Mark 8:38; Isaiah 59:13
speaking against the Lord's anointed*	1 Samuel 26:9–11; Numbers 12; Jude 8; Psalm 105:15; 1 Samuel 24; 2 Samuel 1:16
blasphemy	Mark 7:22; Matthew 15:19; Colossians 3:8
necromancy (trying to commune, call up or talk to the dead)	Deuteronomy 18:11, KJV

Appendix E

Sin	Scripture references (NKJV except where listed)
idolatry **	Ephesians 5:5; Galatians 5:20; 1 Corinthians 6:9; Revelation 21:8, Deuteronomy 18:10–12; Leviticus 19:31; 20:27; Isaiah 2:6; Ezekiel 13:23
blasphemy against the Holy Spirit (the only unforgivable sin)	Matthew 12:31–32

———————— ∿ ————————

__The Lord's anointed__—servants of the Lord, spiritual leaders, etc. (See 1 Chronicles 16:22.)

**__Idolatry__*—These are some of the things that fall under idolatry, which is an abomination to the Lord (Deut. 18:10–12): divination, sorcery, witchcraft, astrology, reading horoscopes, fortune telling, psychics, palm reading, séances, mediums, spiritists, conjuring spells, using tarot cards, reading tea leaves, playing with a Ouija board, hypnosis, telepathy, ESP, good luck charms, crystal balls, zodiac charms, yoga, martial arts (those that invoke supernatural spiritual power), pagan fetishes (objects regarded as having magical powers).[1]

The Ten Commandments

I am the LORD thy God...Thou shalt have no other gods before me.

Thou shalt not make unto thee any graven image, or any likeness of any thing that is in heaven above, or that is in the earth beneath, or that is in the water under the earth.

Thou shalt not take the name of the Lord thy God in vain; for the LORD will not hold him guiltless that taketh his name in vain.

Remember the sabbath day, to keep it holy. Six days shalt thou labour, and do all thy work: But the seventh day is the sabbath of the LORD thy God: in it thou shalt not do any work...

Honour thy father and thy mother: that thy days may be long upon the land which the Lord thy God giveth thee.

Thou shalt not kill.

Thou shalt not commit adultery.

Thou shalt not steal.

Thou shalt not bear false witness against thy neighbour.

Thou shalt not covet thy neighbour's house, thou shalt not covet thy neighbour's wife... nor any thing that is thy neighbour's.

—EXODUS 20:2–3, 7–10, 12–17, KJV, EMPHASIS ADDED

This is my commandment, That ye love one another, as I have loved you.

—JOHN 15:12

APPENDIX F

HEALING SCRIPTURES AND GOD'S PROMISES

Common Questions Answered in Scripture

How are we saved?

That if thou shalt confess with thy mouth the Lord Jesus, and shalt believe in thine heart that God hath raised him from the dead, thou shalt be saved. For with the heart man believeth unto righteousness; and with the mouth confession is made unto salvation.

—ROMANS 10:9–10

What is faith?

Now faith is the substance [assurance] of things hoped for, the evidence of things not seen.

—HEBREWS 11:1

How do we get faith?

So then faith cometh by hearing, and hearing by the word of God.

—ROMANS 10:17

How do we please God?

But without faith it is impossible to please him; for he that cometh to God must believe that he is, and that he is a rewarder of them that diligently seek him.

—HEBREWS 11:6

147

Who is our Healer?

For I am the LORD that healeth thee.

—EXODUS 15:26

Are repentance and forgiveness important for healing?

Confess your faults one to another, and pray one for another that ye may be healed.

—JAMES 5:16

And when ye stand praying, forgive, if ye have ought against any: that your Father also which is in heaven may forgive you your trespasses. But if ye do not forgive, neither will your Father which is in heaven forgive your trespasses.

—MARK 11:25–26

Healing Scriptures

God is our refuge and strength, a very present help in trouble.

—PSALM 46:1

He healeth the broken in heart, and bindeth up their wounds.

—PSALM 147:3

I will extol thee, O LORD; for thou hast lifted me up, and hast not made my foes to rejoice over me. O LORD my God, I cried unto thee, and thou hast healed me.

—PSALM 30:1–2

Is any among you afflicted? Let him pray. Is any merry? Let him sing psalms. Is any sick among you? Let him call for the elders of the church; and let them pray over him, anointing him with oil in the name of the Lord: And the prayer of faith shall save [heal] the sick, and the Lord shall raise him up;

and if he have committed sins, they shall be forgiven him. Confess your faults one to another, and pray one for another, that ye may be healed. The effectual fervent prayer of a righteous man availeth much.

—JAMES 5:13–16

And this is the confidence that we have in him, that, if we ask any thing according to his will, he heareth us: And if we know that he hear us, whatsoever we ask, we know that we have the petitions that we desired of him.

—1 JOHN 5:14–15

Then they cry unto the LORD in their trouble, and he saveth them out of their distresses. He sent his word, and healed them, and delivered them from their destructions.

—PSALM 107:19–20

Jesus said unto him, If thou canst believe, all things are possible to him that believeth.

—MARK 9:23

Blessed is he that considereth the poor: the LORD will deliver him in time of trouble. The LORD will preserve him, and keep him alive; and he shall be blessed upon the earth: and thou wilt not deliver him unto the will of his enemies. The LORD will strengthen him upon the bed of languishing [sickness]: thou wilt make [restore] all his bed in his sickness.

—PSALM 41:1–3

Bless the LORD, O my soul, and forget not all his benefits: Who forgiveth all thine iniquities; who healeth all thy diseases.

—PSALM 103:2–3

My son, attend to my words; incline thine ear unto my sayings. Let them not depart from thine eyes; keep them in the midst of thine heart. For they are life unto those that find them, and health to all their flesh.

—PROVERBS 4:20–22

Hear, O my son, and receive my sayings; and the years of thy life shall be many.

—PROVERBS 4:10

And ye shall serve the LORD your God, and he shall bless thy bread, and thy water; and I will take sickness away from the midst of thee.

—EXODUS 23:25

Behold, I will bring it health and cure [healing], and I will cure them, and will reveal unto them the abundance of peace and truth.

—JEREMIAH 33:6

And Jesus went about all the cities and villages, teaching in their synagogues, and preaching the gospel of the kingdom, and healing every sickness and every disease among the people.

—MATTHEW 9:35

Because thou hast made the LORD, which is my refuge, even the most High, thy habitation; There shall no evil befall thee, neither shall any plague [sickness] come nigh thy dwelling.

—PSALM 91:9–10

Humble yourselves therefore under the mighty hand of God, that he may exalt you in due time: Casting all your care upon him; for he careth for you.

—1 PETER 5:6–7

Trust in the LORD with all thine heart; and lean not unto thine own understanding. In all thy ways acknowledge him,

Appendix F

and he shall direct thy paths. Be not wise in thine own eyes: fear the LORD, and depart from evil. It shall be health to thy navel [body], and marrow [refreshment] to thy bones.

—PROVERBS 3:5–8

The light of the eyes rejoiceth the heart: and a good report maketh the bones fat [healthy/whole].

—PROVERBS 15:30

Pleasant words are as an honeycomb, sweet to the soul, and health to the bones.

—PROVERBS 16:24

Death and life are in the power of the tongue: And they that love it shall eat the fruit thereof.

—PROVERBS 18:21

A merry heart doeth good like a medicine: but a broken spirit drieth the bones.

—PROVERBS 17:22

Surely He hath borne our griefs [sicknesses], and carried our sorrows [pain]: yet we did esteem him stricken, smitten of God, and afflicted. But he was wounded for our transgressions, he was bruised for our iniquities: the chastisement of our peace was upon him; and with his stripes [wounds] we are healed.

—ISAIAH 53:4–5

And he cast out the spirits with his word, and healed all that were sick.

—MATTHEW 8:16

For I will restore health unto thee, and I will heal thee of thy wounds, saith the LORD.

—JEREMIAH 30:17

Submit yourselves therefore to God. Resist the devil, and he will flee from you. Draw nigh to God, and he will draw nigh [near] to you.

—JAMES 4:7–8

For God hath not given us the spirit of fear; but of power, and of love, and of a sound mind.

—2 TIMOTHY 1:7

Beloved, I wish above all things that thou mayest prosper and be in health, even as thy soul prospereth.

—3 JOHN 1:2

Again I say unto you, That if two of you shall agree on earth as touching any thing that they shall ask, it shall be done for them of my Father which is in heaven. For where two or three are gathered together in my name, there am I in the midst of them.

—MATTHEW 18:19–20

Therefore I say unto you, What things soever ye desire, when ye pray, believe that ye receive them, and ye shall have them.

—MARK 11:24

But unto you that fear my name shall the Sun of righteousness arise with healing in his wings.

—MALACHI 4:2

Jesus answered and said unto them, Verily I say unto you, If ye have faith, and doubt not, ye shall not only do this which is done to the fig tree, but also if ye shall say unto this mountain, Be thou removed, and be thou cast into the sea; it shall be done. And all things, whatsoever ye shall ask in prayer, believing, ye shall receive.

—MATTHEW 21:21–22

Appendix F

Heal me, O LORD, and I shall be healed; save me, and I shall be saved: for thou art my praise.

—JEREMIAH 17:14

So shall my word be that goeth forth out of my mouth: it shall not return unto me void [empty], but it shall accomplish that which I please, and it shall prosper in the thing whereto I sent it.

—ISAIAH 55:11

If ye abide in me, and my words abide in you, ye shall ask what ye will, and it shall be done unto you.

—JOHN 15:7

Verily, verily, I say unto you, Whatsoever ye shall ask the Father in my name, he will give it you.

—JOHN 16:23

Ye are of God, little children, and have overcome them: because greater is he [Holy Spirit] that is in you, than he [the devil] that is in the world.

—1 JOHN 4:4

The LORD is my light and my salvation; whom shall I fear? The LORD is the strength of my life; of whom shall I be afraid?

—PSALMS 27:1

Verily, verily, I say unto you, He that believeth on me, the works that I do shall he do also; and greater works than these shall he do; because I go unto my Father. And whatsoever ye shall ask in my name, that will I do, that the Father may be glorified in the Son. If ye shall ask any thing in my name, I will do it. If ye love me, keep my commandments.

—JOHN 14:12–15

Peace I leave with you, my peace I give unto you: not as the world giveth, give I unto you. Let not your heart be troubled, neither let it be afraid.

—JOHN 14:27

When thou liest down, thou shalt not be afraid: yea, thou shalt lie down, and thy sleep shall be sweet.

—PROVERBS 3:24

Be careful [anxious] for nothing; but in every thing by prayer and supplication with thanksgiving let your requests be made known unto God. And the peace of God, which passeth all understanding, shall keep your hearts and minds through Christ Jesus.

—PHILIPPIANS 4:6–7

For if ye live after the flesh, ye shall die: but if ye through the Spirit do mortify the deeds of the body, ye shall live.

—ROMANS 8:13

But they that wait upon the LORD shall renew their strength; they shall mount up with wings as eagles; they shall run, and not be weary; and they shall walk, and not faint.

—ISAIAH 40:31

My son, forget not my law; but let thine heart keep my commandments; For length of days, and long life, and peace, shall they add to thee.

—PROVERBS 3:1–2

(When we give and care for the poor) Then shall thy light break forth as the morning, and thine health shall spring forth speedily; and thy righteousness shall go before thee; the glory of the LORD shall be thy rereward [rear guard/protection].

—ISAIAH 58:8

Appendix F

And I say unto you, Ask, and it shall be given you; seek, and ye shall find; knock, and it shall be opened unto you. For everyone that asketh receiveth; and he that seeketh findeth; and to him that knocketh it shall be opened.

—LUKE 11:9–10

And these signs shall follow them that believe; In my name shall they cast out devils [demons]; they shall speak with new tongues; They shall take up serpents; and if they drink any deadly thing, it shall not hurt them; they shall lay hands on the sick, and they shall recover.

—MARK 16:17–18

But the LORD is faithful, who shall stablish [strengthen] you, and keep you from evil.

—2 THESSALONIANS 3:3

I am fearfully and wonderfully made.

—PSALM 139:14

For the weapons of our warfare are not carnal, but mighty through God to the pulling down of strongholds; Casting down imaginations, and every high [proud] thing that exalteth itself against the knowledge of God, and bringing into captivity every thought to the obedience of Christ.

—2 CORINTHIANS 10:4–5

The spirit of the Lord GOD is upon me; because the LORD hath anointed me to preach good tidings unto the meek; he hath sent me to bind up the broken-hearted, to proclaim liberty to the captives, and the opening of the prison to them that are bound; To proclaim the acceptable year of the LORD, and the day of vengeance of our God; to comfort all that mourn; To appoint unto them that mourn in Zion, to give unto them beauty for ashes, the oil of joy for mourning, the garment of praise for the spirit of heaviness;

that they might be called trees of righteousness, the planting of the LORD, that he might be glorified.

—ISAIAH 61:1–3

Now when the sun was setting, all they that had any sick with divers [various] diseases, brought them unto him; and he laid his hands on every one of them, and healed them.

—LUKE 4:40

Who his own self bare our sins in his own body on the tree, that we, being dead to sins, should live unto righteousness: by whose stripes ye were healed.

—1 PETER 2:24

How God anointed Jesus of Nazareth with the Holy Ghost and with power: who went about doing good, and healing all that were oppressed of the devil; for God was with him.

—ACTS 10:38

And when he had called unto him his twelve disciples, he gave them power against unclean spirits, to cast them out, and to heal all manner of sickness and all manner of disease.

—MATTHEW 10:1

If ye continue in my word, then are ye my disciples indeed; And ye shall know the truth, and the truth shall make you free.

—JOHN 8:31–32

Fear thou not; for I am with thee: be not dismayed; for I am thy God: I will strengthen thee; yea, I will help thee; yea, I will uphold thee with the right hand of my righteousness.

—ISAIAH 41:10

Appendix F

The Promise of God's Protection

He who dwells in the secret place of the Most High Shall abide under the shadow of the Almighty. I will say of the LORD, "He is my refuge and my fortress; My God, in Him I will trust." Surely He shall deliver you from the snare of the fowler and from the perilous pestilence. He shall cover you with His feathers, and under His wings you shall take refuge, His truth shall be your shield and buckler. You shall not be afraid of the terror by night, nor of the arrow that flies by day, nor of the pestilence that walks in darkness, nor of the destruction that lays waste at noonday. A thousand may fall at your side, and ten thousand at your right hand; but it shall not come near you. Only with your eyes shall you look, and see the reward of the wicked. Because you have made the LORD, who is my refuge, even the Most High, your dwelling place, no evil shall befall you, nor shall any plague come near your dwelling; for He shall give His angels charge over you, to keep you in all your ways. In their hands they shall bear you up, lest you dash your foot against a stone. You shall tread upon the lion and the cobra, the young lion and the serpent you shall trample underfoot. Because he has set his love upon Me, therefore I will deliver him; I will set him on high, because he has known My name. He shall call upon Me, and I will answer him; I will be with him in trouble; I will deliver him and honor him. With long life I will satisfy him, and show him my salvation.

—PSALM 91:1–16

NOTES

CHAPTER 8
A FLICKER OF HOPE

1. Merlin R. Carothers, *Power in Praise* (Escondido, CA: Merlin R. Carothers, 1972).

CHAPTER 9
KEYS TO HEALING

1. Merlin R. Carothers, *Prison To Praise* (Escondido, CA: Merlin R. Carothers).
2. Derek Prince, *God's Medicine Bottle* (New Kensington, PA: Whitaker House, 1984).
3. Charles Capps, *God's Creative Power for Healing* (Tulsa, OK: Harrison House, 1976).
4. Francis MacNutt, *Healing* (Notre Dame, IN: Ave Marie Press, 1974).
5. Francis MacNutt, *The Power to Heal* (Notre Dame, IN: Ave Marie Press, 1977).
6. Derek Prince, *Blessing or Curse, You Can Choose* (Grand Rapids, MI: Chosen Books, 1990).
7. Ron G. Campbell, *Free From Freemasonry* (Ventura, CA: Regal Books, 1999).
8. Jack Harris, *Freemasonry, The Invisible Cult in Our Midst* (Springdale, PA: Whitaker House, 1983).
9. Coriden, Green, and Heinstschel, eds, *Commentary on the Code of Canon Law* (Mahwah, N.J.: Paulist Press, 1985), 923.

CHAPTER 10
LEARNING SPIRITUAL WARFARE

1. *The Kansas City Star*, September 6, 2001

CHAPTER 13
THE GLORY REALM IN CHICAGO

1. Benny Hinn, *Good Morning Holy Spirit* (Nashville, TN: Thomas Nelson, Inc., 1990)

CHAPTER 14
DIVINE HELP AT MY MOTHER'S DEATH

1. *Webster's New Collegiate Dictionary* (Springfield, MA: G. & C. Merriam Co., 1977.)
2. *The Catechism of the Catholic Church,* second edition (Libreria Editrice Varticana, 1994), 268: 1030. "All who die in God's grace and friendship, but still imperfectly purified, are indeed assured of their eternal salvation; but after death they undergo purification, so as to achieve the holiness necessary to enter the joy of heaven."

CHAPTER 15
ISRAEL AND THE TRUMAN CONNECTION

1. Rick Joyner, *The Harvest* (New Kensington, PA, Whitaker House, 1989), 176–177.
2. Harry S. Truman, *Memoirs by Harry S. Truman* (The Gallery Press, 1955), 116.
3. William Hillman, *Mr. President* (Farrar, Straus, and Young, 1952), 204.
4. Robert H. Ferrell, *Off the Record: The Private Papers of Harry S. Truman* (New York: Harper and Row, 1980), 252.
5. Michael T. Benson, *Harry S. Truman and the Founding of Israel* (Westport, CT: Praeger, 1997).
6. Alfred Steinberg, *The Man From Missouri: The Life and Times of Harry. S. Truman* (New York: G. P. Putnam and Sons, 1962), 306.
7. Margaret Truman, *Harry S. Truman* (New York: William Morrow and Company, 1972), 389.
8. Alfred Steinberg, *The Man From Missouri: The Life and Times of Harry S. Truman.*
9. Mike Bickle, *Encountering Jesus: Visitations, Revelations, and Angelic Activity*, www.fotb.com.

CHAPTER 17
KNOWLEDGE NEEDED FOR HEALING

1. Mike Bickle, *Growing in the Prophetic* (Lake Mary, FL: Creation House, 1996).

Notes

2. Fr. Thomas Dubay, *Fire Within* (San Francisco, CA: Ignatius Press, 1989), 244–245.
3. Pastor Henry Wright, *A More Excellent Way, A Teaching on the Spiritual Roots of Disease* (Molena, GA: Pleasant Valley Church, Inc., 1999).
4. Derek Prince, *They Shall Expel Demons* (Grand Rapids, MI: Chosen Books, 1998).
5. Francis MacNutt, *Deliverance from Evil Spirits* (Grand Rapids, MI: Chosen Books, 1995).
6. Kenneth E. Hagin, *Words* (Tulsa, OK: RHEMA Bible Church, 1979).

CHAPTER 18
A FEW EXAMPLES OF COMMON OCCULT ART,
FALSE GODS, AND SUPERSTITIONS

1. *The Columbia Electronic Encyclopedia*, sixth edition (Columbia University Press, 2003), s.v. "Buddhism." Available online at www.bartleby.com (accessed March 2004).
2. *Encyclopedia Britannica 2003 Deluxe Edition CD-ROM*, s.v. "cupid."
3. Paul Gambling, *Gargoyle Etymology and History*, www.paulgambling.co.uk (accessed September 2002).
4. Julie LaMay, Ph.D., *The Legends of Kokopelli*, www.drlamay.com/kokopelli.htm (accessed March 2004).
5. *The Columbia Electronic Encyclopedia*, s.v. "fairy, brownie, dwarf, elf, gnome, goblin, leprechaun, pixie."
6. Ibid., s.v. "dragon, snake worship."
7. Ibid., s.v. "sun worship."
8. Ibid., s.v. "unicorn."

APPENDIX A

1. Finis Jennings Dake, *Dake's Annotated Reference Bible* (Lawrenceville, GA: Dake Bible Sales, Inc., 1996), notes on the Book of Malachi, 927.
2. Finis Jennings Dake, *God's Plan for Man* (Lawrenceville, GA: Dake Bible Sales, Inc., 1977). Lesson 17, part VIII.

3. The Jewish calendar in Old Testament times used 360 days (twelve months of 30 days each) to make a year, not the 365.25 days per year that is used today. Thus, for example, 430 biblical years would equate to 423.8 years in today's calendar. For more information see reference 4 below.

4. Grant R. Jeffery, *The Signature of God* (Printed in Canada, Frontier Research Publications, Inc., 2002), chapter 7.

APPENDIX C
SPIRITUAL ROOTS OF DISEASE

1. Pastor Henry Wright, *A More Excellent Way, A Teaching on the Spiritual Roots of Disease* (Molena, GA: Pleasant Valley Church, Inc., 1999.) Roots used by permission of Pastor Henry Wright.

2. Ibid, 145, 223.

APPENDIX D
SPIRITUAL BLOCKS TO HEALING

1. Spiritual blocks from *A More Excellent Way, A Teaching on the Spiritual Roots of Disease* (Molena, GA: Pleasant Valley Church, Inc., 1999.) and from various teaching tapes by Pastor Henry Wright of *Pleasant Valley Church, Inc.*, Thomaston, Georgia. Blocks used by permission of Pastor Henry Wright.

APPENDIX E
SIN: A BLOCK TO HEALING

1. Derek Prince, *Blessing or Curse, You Can Choose* (Grand Rapids, MI: Chosen Books, 1990), chapter 6.

TO CONTACT THE AUTHOR
Mary T. Gracey
P. O. Box 12511
Overland Park, KS 66282-2511
Email: TheHealingWord@kc.rr.com
www.HeLiftedMeUp.com